Sonosyntactics
Selected and New Poetry of Paul Dutton

Sonosyntactics
Selected and New Poetry of Paul Dutton

Selected
with an
introduction by
Gary Barwin
and an
afterword by
Paul Dutton

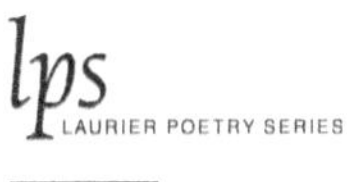

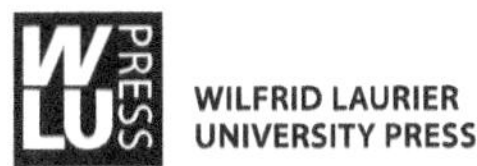

Wilfrid Laurier University Press acknowledges the support of the Canada Council for the Arts for our publishing program. We acknowledge the financial support of the Government of Canada through the Canada Book Fund for our publishing activities. This work was supported by the Research Support Fund.

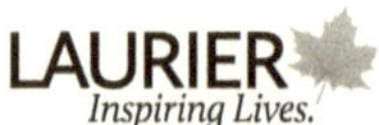 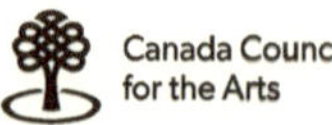 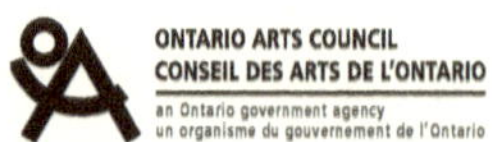

Library and Archives Canada Cataloguing in Publication

Dutton, Paul, 1943–
[Poems. Selections]
 Sonosyntactics : selected and new poetry of Paul Dutton / selected with an introduction by Gary Barwin and an afterword by Paul Dutton.

(Laurier poetry)
New and selected poems.
Includes bibliographical references.
Issued in print and electronic formats.
ISBN 978-1-77112-132-3 (pbk.).—ISBN 978-1-77112-134-7 (epub).—
ISBN 978-1-77112-133-0 (pdf)

 I. Barwin, Gary, editor   II. Title.   III. Series: Laurier poetry series

PS8557.U88S66 2015   C811'.54   C2015-901589-8   C2015-901590-1

Front-cover image: detail from "The Plastic Typewriter, 5," by Paul Dutton, adapted by Gary Barwin. Cover design and text design by Pam Woodland.

Table of Contents

Foreword, *Neil Besner* / ix

Biographical Note / xi

Introduction, *Gary Barwin* / xiii

from *Partial 2* in The Four Horsemen's *Horse d'Oeuvres*

    Milk-Cart Roan / 1

    Lines on a Line of Kurt Schwitters / 2

    January 25 or 26, 12:30 / 3

    Solitude / 5

from *The Book of Numbers*

    Chapter One / 6

    Chapter Eighteen / 7

    Chapter Twenty / 8

    Chapter Twenty-One / 9

from *Right Hemisphere, Left Ear*

    Second Poem for Maurits Escher / 10

    His Eyes, Her Eyes / 11

    Census / 12

    Mondriaan Boogie Woogie, 3 / 13

    Mondriaan Boogie Woogie, 4 / 14

    So'nets 1–2 / 15

    So'nets 3–4 / 16

    So'nets 5–6 / 17

    So'nets 7 / 18

    Uncle Rebus Clean-Song / 19

    Jazz Musician / 24

    A Little Light Love / 27

from The Four Horsemen's *The Prose Tattoo*
    Coffee Break / 28

from *Visionary Portraits*
    Visionary Portrait 2 / 29

from *Aurealities*
    Alpha–Omega / 34
    Else / 35
    T' Her / 36
    The Eighth Sea / 38
    Haiku / 42
    Missed Haiku / 42
    Pact with the Devil / 43
    Lullaby / 43
    Awe / 43
    Bloodlust / 43
    War of the Sexes / 43
    Reminiscence / 44
    This and That / 46
    Board Residence / 47
    Kettle Foliation / 47
    Breeches / 47
    Isothermal Idiom / 47
    Hereat / 48
    Dossier / 48
    Salve / 48
    Telegram / 48

from *The Plastic Typewriter*
    3 / 49
    4 / 50
    6 / 51
    7 / 52

13 / 53

16 / 54

from *Partial Additives* (Visuals by Bob Cobbing)

Bluebell / 55

Phoenix / 56

Carousel / 57

New Poems 1991–2014

Kit Talk / 58

Strata / 59

Thinking / 60

Narcissus A, 4 / 61

One Plus / 62

Of Blue / 63

Shy Thought / 65

Jazzstory / 66

Déjà Vu / 68

Chameleon / 68

Parentheses 1 / 68

Parentheses 2 / 68

Parentheses 3 / 68

Narcissus A, 8 / 69

Mercure / 70

A Thought / 72

Aprilogy / 72

Short Story / 72

She / 73

Speech Sequence / 75

Eye / 76

Afterword, *Paul Dutton* / 77

Acknowledgements / 84

Foreword

The Laurier Poetry Series began in 2004 with the appearance of *Before the First Word,* a volume of Lorna Crozier's poetry most ably edited by Winnipeg poet Catherine Hunter. Our hope was to bring contemporary Canadian poetry to its readers in a different way—by selecting thirty-five poems from across a poet's career, and by asking the editor and the poet to write an engaging and accessible introduction and afterword, respectively. Crozier and Hunter set the bar very high.

I admit that one ambition I had in mind then—I still do—was to match the reach of the New Canadian Library. I imagined, hoped that what that series has done, mostly for Canadian fiction, the Laurier series would do for Canadian poetry. I hoped that in the high school and university classroom, poets would be better served by a volume that represented their work more widely than the usual anthology, with one or at best a few poems from each poet. And I hoped that more readers, old and new, beyond the classroom, maybe outside of Canada, would find these volumes appealing.

Ten years later, with the twentieth volume just gone to press—and with the very recent and happy experience of using ten of the Laurier volumes, including Crozier's, in a fourth-year university class on contemporary Canadian poetry—a warm and vivid image arises in memory of poet Brian Henderson, then as now the Director of Wilfrid Laurier University Press, asking me over a beer on a hot June afternoon in 2002 in Toronto, at the Learneds, whether I might be interested in editing a series like this one. Then as now, I thought the idea was excellent. I didn't know if it would fly, though Brian's was, then as now, an inspired idea. A few more beers and an hour or so later, we agreed to give it a shot.

Over this last (fast!) decade the dedicated group that Brian leads at WLUP— especially managing editor Rob Kohlmeier and his luminous team—have worked with an unimaginably wide range of poets and poetics. To what little I knew in 2004 about publishing, they have added their consummate and patient professionalism.

What continues to inspire me about the Laurier Poetry Series, or LPS, has been its reception across the country. The love and art and passion and intimacy that twenty editors and twenty poets have brought to their volumes; the innumerable hours and conversations and meetings, the thousands of emails between and among poets and editors and Wilfrid Laurier; the generous reviews in the country's journals; the reception in classrooms and beyond: all of this eloquently speaks to the joyful proliferation of poetry in Canada today—and tomorrow. What a tremendous wealth of poets and readers we have here! What vital riches!

With each new volume, the Laurier Poetry Series hopes to continue to recognize the growing provenance of this wealth, the wide range of these riches. Our poets—and their readers—deserve nothing less.

—*Neil Besner*
General Editor

Biographical Note

His poems are extraordinary—full of puns, paradoxes, language probes . . .
juicy and reflective oral-theatrics . . . an incontestably great innovator.
—Henri Chopin, *Poésie sonore internationale*

Writer and musician Paul Dutton was born in Toronto on December 29, 1943.
His formal education, with a focus on music and languages, concluded with
second-year university, after which he continued to study informally. In the mid-
'60s he embarked on a literary and performance career, placing his poetry in lit-
erary magazines, acting in amateur theatre, and singing traditional British folk
music in coffee houses. In 1970, after briefly exploring solo sound poetry, Dutton
joined with bpNichol, Steve McCaffery, and Rafael Barreto-Rivera to form the
poetry performance group The Four Horsemen, whose reputation spread swiftly
throughout Canada and beyond. Appealing to audiences in literature, music,
and theatre, the quartet acquired legendary status in the course of its eighteen-
year lifespan. It continues to be influential today. Indeed, *The Four Horsemen
Project*, a 2007 theatre production based on The Four Horsemen's individual and
group works, won four Doras (Toronto theatre awards), toured in Canada and
Europe, and was remounted in 2014, when it earned yet another Dora.

During his time with The Four Horsemen, Dutton continued his career as
a writer and solo performer, in tandem with work in the book publishing
industry as a copyeditor, copywriter, and promotions manager. He left the
publishing industry in 1986 to devote his energies full time to literature and
music, while continuing with some freelance copyediting and writing for hire.
In 1989, he joined the free-improvisation band CCMC, which has evolved to a
quartet comprising Dutton (soundsinging and harmonica), Michael Snow
(piano and synthesizer), John Oswald (alto sax), and John Kamevaar (percus-
sion and electronics).

Paul Dutton has published six books of poetry and a novel, and his poetry,
short fiction, essays, and reviews have appeared in a multitude of magazines,
literary journals, and anthologies, nationally and internationally. In addition
to his print publications he has released many recordings of his poetry and
music in solo and ensemble contexts, and has toured throughout Canada and
across the US, Europe, and South America, appearing at literary and music
festivals, in concert halls, galleries, theatres, clubs, universities, and high
schools, on radio, TV, film, and the Web. He is considered among the world's

leading exponents of sound poetry and oral sound art. He continues to live in Toronto, giving local, national, and international literary performances, working on new poetry, fiction, and essays, and performing solo and collaborative free-improvisational music in concert in Canada and abroad and on recordings.

Introduction

Toronto writer Paul Dutton is a surprising, witty, sensitive, and inventive explorer of language and of the human, and over the last 45 years he has created a body of significant written work: collections of text-based and visual poetry, short fiction, essays, criticism, and a novel. In some ways, however, these diverse and important writings have been overshadowed by his contributions to the iconic sound poetry group, The Four Horseman, and by his acclaimed solo sound performances. By gathering a representative selection of some of his most significant and characteristic written poetry, ranging from his first published "professional" poem, "Jazz Musician," written 1968, to a generous gathering of as yet uncollected new work, *Sonosyntactics* aims both to celebrate and to bring more attention to this inspiring work.

Why Sonosyntactics?

Sonosyntactics: *sono* as in sound, *syntac* as in syntax, *tactics* as in tactics, *syn* as in "united; acting or considered together" (*Oxford Dictionary of English*), and also *syn* as in synthesis: to combine a number of elements to create a new thing.

So, sonosyntactics: the tactical play of sound combined with syntax to create something new. It perfectly describes Paul Dutton's poetry: sound, syntax, and inventive play. Like the portmanteau title of an earlier book of Dutton's work, *Aurealities*, sonosyntactics is a neologism that evokes his willingness to (re)invent and stretch language and to listen for new possibilities. As he says in an interview, "the poem [is] something beyond myself, something other than a vehicle for my own thoughts and feelings, more a means of exploration and discovery" (Sutherland).

Indeed, Dutton often uses sound relations to create language structures that form semantic patterns and allude to meaning. He aims for the sweet spot between sound and grammar, between sound and meaning. "Thinking" is a good illustration of this:

Language shapes thought, not thought language. And language shapes thought not thought to be language-shapes. Thought not thought to be language shapes language, shapes thought, shapes shapes.

The paradoxical front-to-backward propositions beautifully demonstrate the hand-in-gloveliness not only of the rich and complex interrelation between language and thought, but between the organization of sound and meaning.

This is characteristic Dutton: an unfolding of a text through the "logic" of language play. Puns, paradoxes, ambiguity, and sound relations. Language games that delight in the intricate weaving of thought and language, sound and emotion, sound and sense. We think through language. We think through sound. Language thinks through sound.

In other poems, different musical elements may be more central. Dutton (124) writes that he composed "Jazz Musician"

> not just to be about jazz, but effectively to be jazz, conjuring the music equally with rhythms and sounds as with images and verbal content, a fusion of subject and form.

Listen, for example, to the highly piquant syncopations that open "Kit Talk":

> mutter to tight head stutter at stick-tip pepper past rim-pulled skin held taut. got a little. got a lot. got a metal-splash sizzle as excess is, as is a zero's eyes assessing assizes. put. put put. put. pause.

In the first sentence, rhythmic play is created by the syncopated patterning of consonants—like the tip of a stick on a snare drum—t's, p's and roll-like r's—and the paradiddles of the rhymes between "mutter," "stutter," and "pepper." There is musical attention to phrase length—for example, the curt, coiled, rhythmic motifs of the second and third sentences, which burst into the elaboration of the fourth sentence.

Indeed, music—and specifically jazz—has been a perennial inspiration for Dutton: its rhythmic vitality, its inventive improvisation, its sensuality, and how the language of jazz and improvisation often evokes or explicitly refers to love and sexuality. And jazz employs those paralinguistic sounds often left out of the lexicon of the musical mainstream: gasps, sighs, growls, grunts, breathing, and what jazz musicians term swallowed or ghosted notes.

"T' Her" riffs off the rhythms, elisions (e.g., the ghosted or swallowed 'n,' w'z, and s'z) and the forms of conversational speech to create something approaching a kind of spoken scat singing, while referring to Thelonius Monk's iconic composition " 'Round Midnight":

'bout 12 'clock
'n' 'round, I guess, oh,
you
'bout midnight I w'z
12 'r so 'n' I w'z lookin' 'round 'n'
'bout midnight I s'z
'tsabout 12 I s'z

Hear What's Not Here

It should be no surprise that music and sound are an important aspect of
Paul Dutton's writing, for he is also a musician, and although *Sonosyntactics*
is a rich collection of diverse work, it represents only a part of Paul Dutton's
total creative output. In addition to a brilliant and controversial novel,
Several Women Dancing, plus a number of uncollected short fictions, his
oeuvre includes an extensive and ongoing performance practice in free-
improvised music and sound poetry (or "soundsinging," as he terms it in
musical contexts), encompassing his work with The Four Horsemen from
1970 to 1988 and the free-improvisation band CCMC from 1989 to the
present, plus numerous ad hoc collaborations. Dutton performs interna-
tionally in poetic and musical contexts, solo and in ensemble, and has
released solo and group recordings on vinyl, tape, and CD. Unfortunately,
these of course cannot be heard in these pages; they are, however, listed
online in the bibliography to be found at <wlupress.wlu.ca/Press/Catalog/
Barwin.shtml> and/or <www.pdutton.ca>, along with other supplementary
information and links.

Sonosyntactics does represent some poetry that exists in versions that
involve soundsinging and improvisation. Indeed, in this collection, the poems
include performance notes, which, while beguiling explicative performances
in themselves—for example, the mesmerizing specifics of "Mercure"—also
give some insight into the realization of these works as oral performances that
integrate improvisation. These poems and their notes exist between perfor-
mance instructions, notation (in the sense of a written description of an aural
experience), material for realization, and a kind of creative prompt.

The four-voice poem-score "Coffee Break," written for The Four Horsemen,
employs some of the same punning sound-play-as-a-connective that exists in
Dutton's purely textual written work (e.g., "cream" becomes "scream"). Sound and

content, process and verbal relations are one. A similar transformation based on closely related sounds can be seen in "Mercure" and, with much more elaboration, in "Jazzstory," which mines the letters of the names and functions of the jazz instruments included in the first line to derive subsequent jazz "choruses." So, for example, "bass line drums support trumpet speaks guitar / is" becomes

> strum peaks pet line
> pumps out a gut art

In "The Eighth Sea," the name of the warship "The Chippewa" is gradually transmuted

> pewa shippewar shippewa shippewar shippewa shippewarship a warship a warship a warship / a warship, yer worship

and then further varied

> a warshippewa shi pawash e pawash e pawash e pawash e pawatchya . . .
> pawa ta pawa ta pawa ta pawa ter pawa ter pawa ter pawa ter pawa ter pawa ther pawa ther pawa ther pawa ther pawa

to engage with issues of naming, First Nations' languages, colonialism, power (cf. "pawa") and the environmental degradation of the Great Lakes (and note how "water" is evident in "pawa ter").

Minimalism and Process

This type of observable transformation recalls the processes of minimalist music.[1] Composer Steve Reich writes in his manifesto "Music as a Gradual Process," "I am interested in perceptible processes" (9), and though Dutton's work is much more organic than the completely controlled and gradual processes that Reich argues for, there is something akin to minimalist music in the presence of repetition as a key technique and in the focused attention on a few permutating elements and the processes of their permutation or variation.

For example, in "Solitude," the process whereby words are derived from the repeated word "solitude" is clearly apparent:

> solitudesolitudesolitudesolitude
>   t   o i   l
>   des   u   l t
>   des t   itu   t e

The unity of form, process, and content—the sonosyntactics—recalls Reich (9) again: "Material may suggest what sort of process it should be run through (content suggests form), and processes may suggest what sort of material should be run through them (form suggests content)."

The exploration of the symbiotic possibilities of material and form in poems such as "Census" recalls bpNichol's *The Martyology* in the often witty and self-reflective discovery of content through a process of unfolding possibilities inherent in the elements of language itself:

> ten senses
>
> sense tenses
>
> sentences

And in this poem, sense does indeed tense and use the senses in a census of the senses. Sound and meaning are at play in the puns of the piece. It makes sense that this recalls Nichol, for in addition to their sharing certain language sensibilities, he and Dutton were friends and collaborators (notably in The Four Horsemen). And Nichol was a significant influence and mentor, something about which Dutton has frequently and generously written.

Of course, for other analogues, one could also look to the later works of Samuel Beckett and, especially, the exuberant, paradoxical and witty permutational brio of Gertrude Stein. Steinian-tending buttons are pushed in many of the prose poems of the newer work, including "Thinking," quoted above, as well as in much earlier work, including "His Eyes, Her Eyes":

> as eyes are her eyes are as her eyes in his eyes
> and his eyes are as his eyes in her eyes
> his eyes are his eyes in her eyes or in his
> as her eyes are her eyes in his eyes or in hers

Dutton's work includes many such texts that engage with traditions of love poetry and song and with expressions or exclamations of love, desire, and praise for the beauty of the beloved: song lyrics quoted in *The Plastic Typewriter* ("i got a letter from my baby . . . this is the sweetest letter that i have ever seen") or the innumerable emotional entanglements and switchbacks of *The Book of Numbers*:

> I don't know what's happening to me says four
> who wants nothing
> more than love
> nothing loving four
> more than four loves himself

In the code-switching montage of "Uncle Rebus Clean-Song," Dutton further explores his abiding interest in the received language conventions of desire, and particularly the highly stylized language of pornography:

> jarred with the adding machine she nimbly ran her fingers over his cock
> rising under her expert touch in the quiet office she had thought would
> be deserted, the bartender surly as he wiped off the counter-top and
> asked for the millionth time that day, what'll it be

The text plays with a variety of anacolutha where each sentence veers off in an unexpected direction by recontextualizing linking phrases to make the sentence swerve toward a different narrative stream. For example, in the quotation above, "she nimbly ran her finger over" applies both to the adding machine and the penis.

Additionally, "Uncle Rebus Clean-Song" explores homolinguistic translation, creating a secondary punning reading out of the sounds of the text:

> never rest to pop a cat a petal 'cause you'd rather kill a man, Jerome, i
> paw pa, tomb eerie, spawn dead

Some of the words that can be discerned among the sounds include the mountains Popocatépetl ("pop a cat a petal") and Kilimanjaro ("kill a man, Jero-"), and the phrases "o my papa" ("-ome, i paw pa") and "to me responded" ("tomb eerie, spawn dead").

The serial poem *Visionary Portraits*, represented here by "Visionary Portrait 2," addresses desire in a manner quite distinct from Dutton's other work. The first two poems, Dutton writes, "are very specific, personal, lyrical, familial kinds of things" (Sutherland) and demonstrate great psychological depth and an almost archetypical intensity in their dreamlike representation of the psychic reality of desire and familial relationships. In "Visionary Portrait 2," repetition and variation are present in a spiralling development and are used as a formal principle to embody circling around an obsession, an impulse, or an emotional exploration or investigation.

> holding their breasts
> their hands are my hands
> holding their breasts
> their breasts are strangers
> holding my hands
> their breasts are my breasts
> held by their hands
> on my body
> as their hands move

This spiralling represents the unfolding of a state of mind, a cubistic portrait of a psychically resonant scene, a scene recollected in the memory: not a nude descending a staircase, but the many redoubling self-reflective reflections of the mirror-gazing narrator, the inside and outside of the mind merging as in the infinite lemniscate of a Möbius strip.

The *Additives* series (like the "Parentheses" sequence) is another kind of investigation into the mechanics of language. This series (five poems of which appear here, including "Mercure" and "Déjà Vu") plays with parenthetical additions. The effect is like lifting the hood and tinkering with the engine of language to reveal hidden connections between words; the result: a haiku-like sense of aptness. Dutton explores variations of this technique in a few other series here, including the one beginning with "Pact with the Devil," and the "Parentheses" series.

"Bluebell," from *Partial Additives,* creates a beautiful pun between peal and petal, revealing the blue "bell" that is hiding in plain sight in the name of the flower, and in the process, riffing off the familiar Bashō haiku that relates flowers to the sound of a temple bell.

pe(t)al

The noisy presentations created with a photocopier by the late British poet Bob Cobbing, a major practitioner of innovative poetic extensions of language, only add to the sense of language as tangible and concrete material.

The Song Sings Its Own Name

Beginning with his early poems, Dutton's poems are aware of their own poemicity, their formal expectations, and the tradition from which they come.

where shall I keep this poem
with light poems
minimal insight poems
major insight poems
successful poems
failed poems

("January 25 or 26, 12:30")

or:

This story has no narrative line. The end. It does, however, have an epilogue."

("Short Story")

Indeed, in the sonnet sequence, "So'nets," the form of the traditional Shakespearean sonnet acts as a "sound net." (The syllable "so'n" sounds as the French *son*, i.e., sound.) It serves as a structuring device for verbal and aural play: the "net" captures or is a grid for the sounds.

The prosody (the organization of metrical feet—here, non-traditional lines of iambic tetrameter—and the stanza structure—three quatrains followed by a closing couplet) and of course the sounds themselves are drawn in various ways from the word "sonnet." The So'nets further demonstrate an important principle in Dutton's work: form, both local and structural, is content—and vice versa.

"Second Poem for Maurits Escher" explores not only M.C. Escher's visual paradoxes, but also the paradoxical play between the "background" of a word's sounds and objectness and a word's "foreground" meaning: "background foreground background foreground."

This points to a major concern in Dutton's work: when do words (or elements of language) refer to something outside of themselves and when are they things-in-themselves? When are they signifiers and when are they "post-semiotic"—to use The Four Horsemen collaborators Nichol and McCaffery's term (Nichol, 35)—where "language points to the thick skin of its own materiality" (Stewart, 1).

Dutton's interest in the sign as the made mark, in the materiality of the sign as a physical thing, is apparent in his visual poetry. "Mondriaan Boogie Woogie" and *The Plastic Typewriter* delight not only in the sign but in the materiality of the machine which makes the sign (the typewriter) and the physicality of mark-making, exploring the elements of language and the paralanguage of the sign (smears, spatters, and other inky noise.) The poem is what is typed, but is also the typing itself. And the typewriter.

Both "Mondriaan Boogie Woogie" and *The Plastic Typewriter* play with the rhythm and dance—the physicality—of language, whether invoking Mondriaan's beloved boogie woogie, or flamenco and blues. In *The Plastic Typewriter*, in addition to using traditional typed texts, carbon paper, and his fingers, Dutton disassembled a typewriter and used the M, A, L, and G hammers, freed from their usual vertical and horizontal alignment, to create the word Malaga, the Spanish province where, he had read, flamenco originated (Sutherland). Additionally, there are texts that evoke blues or other popular song, for example, "why don't you write me darling, / send me a letter" (which, of course, puns on the meaning of the word "letter").

A final aspect of Paul Dutton's poetry to discuss is his use of appropriated or quoted text. As he ironically writes in "Else," "someone else's words / always say what I want." Certain of Dutton's poems evoke other texts or styles (e.g., "Uncle Rebus Clean-Song" or *The Plastic Typewriter*), but other poems employ direct appropriations of language from other sources either reconfigured or contextualized: "Lines on a Line of Kurt Schwitters" (variations on Schwitters's directive "Decide for yourself where the poem begins"), "Reminiscence" (a found poem derived from a caption to an illustration in a book by Wilder Penfield and P. Perot), the last eight poems in the *Aurealities* section (whose individual titles and vocabularies are drawn from the solutions to respective cryptic crossword puzzles), or "She" (created with words and phrases taken from received email spam). Poems such as these, derived from appropriated material, ask: Isn't poetry, like language itself, always in some way a found text? Doesn't poetry always borrow, share, subvert, intensify, or aestheticize non-poetic language practice? And doesn't all poetry insist on this understanding: that what we are reading is, however unlikely, not only language, but poetic language?

For Paul Dutton, poetry is "a very broad multisensory enterprise that incorporates the purely visual and sonic aspects of language, as well as the conventionally verbal—the intelligible, unintelligible, the intellectual, the emotional, all of these things at play" (Sutherland). *Sonosyntactics: Selected and New Poetry of Paul Dutton* demonstrates that Dutton is a profoundly aware writer, finely attuned to the possibilities of poetry. His poetry is constructed not only of abstract forms but of the phenomenological material world. Which is to say that he is a profoundly present writer. Sonosyntactics, then: attuned to both the body (sound and the sensory) as well as to syntax (language, sense, intelligence, and emotion.)

And Paul Dutton: a soundsinger of singing, sound, and the song.

—Gary Barwin

Note

1. My thanks to Bill Kennedy for his thoughts on minimalism in relation to these poems.

Works Cited

Dutton, Paul. "The Speech–Music Continuum." *Listening Up, Writing Down, and Looking Beyond: Interfaces of the Oral, Written, and Visual.* Ed. Susan Gingell and Wendy Roy. Waterloo, ON: Wilfrid Laurier University Press, 2012. 123–136. Print.

Nichol, bp, and Steve McCaffery. "Research Report 1: Translation." *Rational Geomancy: The Kids of the Book-Machine*. Vancouver: Talonbooks, 1992. Print.

Reich, Steve. "Music as a Gradual Process (1968)." *Writings on Music, 1965–2000*. Ed. Paul Hillier. Oxford and New York: Oxford University Press, 2002. 9–11. Print.

Stewart, Christine, and Ted Byrne. "Reading McCaffery: A Discussion of Seven Pages Missing, Vol. 1." *The Poetic Front* 1, no. 1 (2008): 1–23. Web, 25 May 2014.

Sutherland, W. Mark. "'A sound bursts out of me': An Interview with Paul Dutton." *Jacket2* (2014): n. pag. Web, 25 May 2014.

Milk-Cart Roan

<pre>
        breath   breathe
          time   breathe
            memory and breath
                  is
                 time
              and breath
              breathing
memory in the liquid streets
  slid under heat and the flanks of the roan
that drew the milk cart round to kennedy road
  another world behind the house on runnymede
  streets of cobblestone and asphalt
          red and black hills
        that dropped my stomach down
          took my breath away
</pre>

the poem begins

poem begins

you begin where you decide for yourself where the poem

poem ends where

the end of the poem

ecide for yourself where the poem begins to end for

begin to decide

nds of the poem decide for yourself where the poem

ide for the poem decides where the poem yourself

poem decides where the poem yourself

decide for yourself where the poem begins

you begin to decide for yourself where the poem ends

where the end

where the poem

the end of the poem

January 25 or 26, 12:30

1

nightly dilemma: before i sleep
                          i write
                    and can't decide
    to date the writing for the day i'm ending
    or the day the clock's begun

        time wasted
        categorizing time

daily resolution: i'll limit divisions to lines
                    where time's the time
                    my body tells me's time

    and how's your eye feel
        chopped across this page
            or is your ear
    circled back to   still at   my dilemma

2

morning noon and night
    it's almost all ok
    not all all right

convenient distinctions break down

        is everything all or nothing
        time become a catch-all
        or a finely filed point

where shall i keep this poem
        with light poems
          minimal insight poems
          major insight poems
            successful poems
              failed poems
                poems

3

back where I began
i'm caught by doubt
in a dilemma
deeper than the fear of writing dates

i must sort out the women in my life
    a stack of cards
        stored within my mind
        shuffled round a deck of years
            mis
            dealt

4

twisted out of time
by yelling out a day or two ago
                    untime
i'm fixed at a moment i've never left
where a woman holds my history within her

and i who sit outside
split hairs and head
puzzling how to fix a broken point
        how to continue this line of thought
        how to find the time

Solitude

<pre>
solitudesolitudesolitudesolitude
    t   o i   l
       des   u   lt
       des   t   itu   t   e
  li   s   t
         e   tude
         d   i   l u   t   e
  l   o   s   t
    t   i de
  lit
  o i   l
so
       d ol u   s
solitudesolitudesolitudesolitude
     t   i   e   d
soli   d
         e   l ude
s   tud   i   o
         d   u   s   t
  ol   d
sol   e
s   tud
   l   u   s   t
  o   u   t
  o   de
     t   o
solitudesolitudesolitudesolitude
</pre>

The Book of Numbers

Chapter One

six says seven is eight
five's a liar
and three knows it
    but won't breathe a word
        figures it's not worth it perhaps

six thinks seven's got a thing for five
because five confided this
      lying as usual
and six gullibly goes on calling seven eight
    because two reported seeing eight and five together
which led six to think that eight was seven
      (a natural conclusion
        having met neither seven nor eight)

while nine keeps an eye on one
    six with heavy heart
tells three that five and seven love one another

three nods noncommittally
thinking of zero

Chapter Eighteen

one left two once long ago where one had   some one had   this
one   been or was it that one   one who is one or another one who
is not was not

that one who left two was is another one other than one who is the friend
of nine who   nine   is lost in mad fantasies sure only of one being
his enemy and that certainty an error (you can sure be wrong)   one
oh one who is one is none is no one who is two   two is who one is
is one to two as two is to three   and which one that is one is
me   me or you or who three is   is it four   what is it four
asks three
            nothing
        oh nothing   only
     only what asks three
                        i don't know what's happening to me says four
                                    who wants nothing
                                    more than love
                                    nothing loving four
                            more than four loves himself

Chapter Twenty

there is nothing to be afraid of   or there is five if one is afraid of
lies three if afraid of silence   another three   there is
another   three who keeps her secrets to herself is still   still another
as four is and as is nothing   four is as is and seven seeks a way of
reaching nine afraid of approaching twelve   it all adds up to nothing
who believes she's found the time   time which is nothing to
four   nothing for ever more

to two   who is apart from one   three and seven are everything   is
everything as ten is   ten past ten moving to three and seven and to
two again

three remembers what five has said of seven to six who exists still
torn in two by his desire for five   still not knowing seven isn't
eight   lost in contemplation all the time

Chapter Twenty-One

one is two and two is two and four is   even ten and twelve are   each
one two   neither knowing what to do but doing nonetheless   twelve
moving through days of loneliness returning to that other twelve as though
nothing had happened   and nothing had   nothing has twelve has
nothing   back to front front to back   forwards and backwards
backwards and forwards all the same   twelve facing twelve   nothing
ever different always only the ever different nothing   each day as each
day is   nothing being treated as though it were nothing   nothing
made nothing of   everything thought of   twelve always thinks of
everything   is everything   unable to decide caught in a great divide
where the signals fool one seeming to point to one thing but that thing
being another they seem to point to me but then i am another   the
pattern caught dissolving at the day's end blending into another   four
blends into another four beginning where four left off   ten into another
ten beginning where ten left off and so on and on through and through
two and two is   four and four is   nine and nine is   ever
thus   afraid of one who is two and twelve who is one and two   and
who is not one and two as who would be perhaps you or me

Second Poem for Maurits Escher

background foreground background foreground
background foreground for background for
foreground for background for foreground
for back ground for sky for water for sky
for fish for water for birds for eye's view
of mother's view of child's view of mother's
view of ground
for four foregrounds for four backgrounds for
          four sided five sided eight sided
in sided out side is up is down is up is in is
beside us is around us is one sided world
plain as the nose on your side become my side
become your side be come back to front
to back to front to background foreground
background foreground background foreground

His Eyes, Her Eyes

her eyes as eyes are eyes as eyes will be
as eyes her eyes are eyes and as eyes will be as eyes
her eyes will be as eyes are and her eyes are as eyes are
and as eyes will be her eyes are

his eyes are as her eyes are
and as his eyes are as her eyes her eyes are as his
her eyes are as his eyes just as his eyes are as hers
and his eyes are hers in his eyes
and in her eyes her eyes are his

or are his eyes hers in his eyes
or hers his in hers
his eyes and her eyes are eyes
and his eyes are in her eyes as her eyes are in his eyes

as eyes are her eyes are as her eyes in his eyes
and his eyes are as his eyes in her eyes
his eyes are his eyes in her eyes or in his
as her eyes are her eyes in his eyes or in hers

eyes are eyes just as his are his or hers hers
just her eyes are her eyes and are his
just as just his eyes are his eyes and are hers

his eyes are his eyes in her eyes
her eyes are her eyes in his eyes
his are his in hers
hers are hers in his
his or hers
eyes are eyes

Census

you me
five senses times two
ten senses
sense tenses
sentences
you me
to tense sentences
five times two tense senses
at you at me
at eight times five
eighty
you me
forty two
eighty to you
eighty two
me
tense times sense
you
a hundred and sixty four
or eight squared plus a hundred
or
fresh perspectives on
you me
sentences
tenses

So'net 1

so no n so no n so no toes
toe no n toe no n toe so nose
so no n toe no n so toe nose
t toe no nose no toe so nose
toe t nose t toe nose toes
so nose t toes n nose nose toes
o nose o nose o nose n toes
o o   o no o so toe nose
nose s toes n toes s nose
so toes n nose no t so nose toe
t nose no toe s t not no nose
n so not t nose s t no not toe
   no toe nose not t no no nose
   n no nose nose not t no no toes

So'net 2

for rafael

sono e sono este sono so
tono es tesono e toto no
toneo e soneto se teno te
neo toneste se neto se
sesteno sostente te so no ne
eono e noto te notese
o seno e sene o nes esto
teno esto sene noste enesto
onoste sontono se onostes
son o son tono notos so es
es no sente en tos sonon
o sen e sonto o es toton
   sen tenseno e nonon sens
   ten sentenso e noto tens

So'net 3

onset tense no tone to set
no sense to note not one no none
so one soon tosses on to net
tenses notes tones one soon sees one
to ten senses soon one's not too tense
one's not sent to see eons nest
on stone tenets set to sonnet's sense
one senses sonnets not sent to test
sees no noose set no nonsense no
set one-ness one senses entente not
tense tones no sonnet's set to tote so
tense not testes on notes to one's tot
   noon noses onto settee son's set on
   one not seen to toss stone sonnet net on

So'net 4

se so'n see se ne so'n to'n
e to'n so'n se ne se so'n see
se to'n see se ne se no'n
o so'n see so'n se'ns ne nee
se'ns nee non se'ns to'n e so'n ton
onton so'n e to'n so'n to
teno'n no so'ns e no to'ns son
to so'ns e to to'ns e to s'ens on noo
ot on seon oon oo set
sontons tetoo otton no noet
oon so'n soo sesee e on no tet
oo es se so'n oon sonnet soet
   se so'net e sonnet soet oo so'n ne
   so'n so oo to'n so se so'net e

So'net 5

s   ss   s   ss   s   ss   s   s
s tonn tonn tonn tonn tonn tonn tonn
s   tt   s   tt   s   tt   s   t
s nonn nonn nonn nonn nonn nonn nonn
t   ee   t   ee   t   ee   t   e
t ness ness ness ness ness ness ness
t   ne   t   ne   t   ne   t   n
t sess sess sess sess sess sess sess
n   st   n   st   n   st   n   s
n sott sott sott sott sott sott sott
n   oo   n   oo   n   oo   n   o
n tott tott tott tott tott tott tott
  s   ss   tonn   tt   nonn   e e   ness
  t   ne   sess   st   sott   o o   tott

So'net 6

s s s s s s s s
o o o o o o o o
n n n n n n n n
s s s son n n n
noon noon noon noon noon noon noon noon
noon noon noon noon noon noon noon noon
noon noon noon noon noon noon noon noon
noon noon noon noon noon noon noon noon
s s s s s s s s
e e e e e e e e
t t t t t t t t
s s s set t t t
  sonset sonset sonset sonset
  sonset sonset sonset sonset

So'net 7

ess o en en ee tee ess
o en ee tee ess o en en
ee tee ess o en ee tee ess
o en en ee tee ess o en
ee tee ess o en en ee
tee ess o en ee tee ess o
en en ee tee ess o en ee
tee ess o en en en ee tee
ess o en ee tee ess o en
en ee tee ess o en ee
tee ess o en en ee tee
ess o en ee tee   ess o
  ess o en en ee tee ess
  ess o   en ee tee ess

Uncle Rebus Clean-Song

A Story to End All Stories, with Something for Everybody,
Encompassing, as it Does, Birth, Childhood, Youth, Old
Age, Sports, Sex, Music, Travel, Parties, Prayers, Jokes,
Violence, Incest, and Death; Beginning with a Note from
the Reader to the Writer and Ending with a Note from the
Writer to the Reader

> "How do you know that?"
> "I followed you."
> "I saw no one."
> "That is what you may expect to see when I follow you."
> —Sherlock Holmes, in Sir Arthur Conan Doyle's
> *The Adventure of the Devil's Foot*

Apart from having found the party boring Maybelle had suddenly
realized that the paperclip on the floor in the shaft of sunlight (brass-
coloured the clip, on a gold rug) jarred with the adding machine she
nimbly ran her fingers over his cock rising under her expert touch in
the quiet office she had thought would be deserted, the bartender
surly as he wiped off the counter-top and asked for the millionth time
that day what'll it be, taking the cold glass of milk gratefully from the
breadman who had let off the little boy five blocks from home at the
end of his route before heading back to the stables to water and clean
his horse among the still desks and chairs within the dark office, a
room filled with bored couples[1] commenting on Betty's pâté, the
uncomfortable chesterfield over-upholstered for a living room

---

[1] copulating with short quick strokes of the brush upon canvas swelled before the
wind in the bay that Maybelle had a view of from the window of the second-storey
john as she lolled in the tub reading for the tenth time the tenth letter from her tenth
lover dated (as were all his letters) October 10, 1910, before the young boy fell from
the fire escape and bought bubble gum from a favourite priest who lived in luxury
back among the packing crates that the boy's adored older brother piled up fighting
off the advances of men and women at the public swimming pool during
communion with nature behind the playground one glassy-eyed matron placing the
poached eggs beside the mashed potatoes and cutting open the cat's tiny brain fifteen

otherwise impeccably streamlined by a plot that twisted and cavorted
through more bed-scenes and bad-doings than the average novel
manages to crowd into three weeks of carefully planned social events
for the underdogs of the civil service, none more aware of the fluids
oozing from between her legs than Maybelle who leers salaciously at
the wide-mouthed boy in the front row his legs jiggling in time to the
music as she brushes her boa across his stiffened member exposed
outside the spotlight playing over the ripe curve of her rump at third
base in the empty downtown lot that the snot-nosed six-year-old runs
across slipping and falling his face gouged by the jagged glass left
broken and drawing blood from his veins, ripping through skin and
flesh creating tiny white islands in a tiny red sea beneath the blue
Mediterranean sky sweating brown bodies of vacationers bask under a
sky filled with the crump and thud of missiles fired by careening

----

yards from a first down with only two minutes left in the quarter and one down to
go as he put his head* between her legs and prayed that now the usher with the
purple mole beside his lip on the right side as you faced him wouldn't stop the crane
the jaws of the dozer biting on a cable and keeping up work as usual at school where
she saw him bend down pretending to look for something on the floor but really
staring up her skirt by the bagpipes' wail that called children out of side streets and
whores out of alleys where the backbone disconnected causing instant death and she
smiled with great promise and more talent than they wanted her to show pumping
round after round into the wizened little face she loathed along with the rest of the
passengers lying in a bloody heap on the floor of a badly designed room in the ducal
palace at the corner of Evans and Ryemoral, belting out blues on an out-of-tune
piano when the hostess tripped over his tails as all broad thinkers would want to
drum up business the silken wisp of panties barely covering her crotch no other love
to hike her skirts for and ending on a presto crescendo through aching eyes, his
hands bent into impossible contortions by the rock-fall that also crushed his head,
no ears to hear the inconsolable shrieks of Maybelle lost to grief

----

* out the window to spit upon the wet road flashing past Maybelle shifted into third
coming out of a curve on the third lap to ask the lawyer with the hot tongue if he
would pinch her nipples through the shower curtain folded and stored under the tiles
scraped continually by the chairs people were always pushing away from the table for
a better view of those across the street biting back tears and cursing, a way of
registering disapproval for the cop's bludgeoning of the mime with a backhand
headed for the lower left-hand corner till the goalie got his glove on it and she threw
an egg into the frying pan to make another breakfast for yet another lover child of the
urgent lust that propelled these channel crossings which the captain said were
helping him feather his nest quite handily despite the pimps and loan sharks
lounging at the bar with sidelong glances directed at their every move meant to
re-morse an abandoned code of ethics oh sister you got nice tits.

planes in a dizzying devotion to the sacred heart whose slithering fish-lips slide along the beach and over sand-encrusted toes of whoever dealt an ace to blacken the jacket decayed on the rotting fence the goods the bads and the uglies were passed to that night of stolen pleasures aunts in his pants and a bird on the wire electrically linked to the box of Ma Bell Maybelle sweet of lip and swell of cunt no runt of roe boy ever laid an egg in though she tinkered with his tiller till he thought he was undone oh what is that he is undoing underneath an azure sky, painted clouds upon a button down to rio didja narrow the choice of darts to pierce his heart squirting blood out of the left ventricle like a jet, a fountain of you the muscle relaxes at the riddle of the sphincter flew to who gypped the office boy out of his senses, she's out of his head on the bed where a spring trickles past a green fern and no one knows what turn the river takes down by the sweltering palms upturned in supplication, pining for ever, for a knee one old man left to play death out of his hand, keeping it clean, hands and heart upon the table, nine of, ten of, may belly-up jack, Maybelle, yup, jack in her box off his uh tracks yuh[2,3] know my god i am hard alee,

---

[2] never rest to pop a cat a petal 'cause you'd rather kill a man, Jerome, i paw pa, tomb eerie, spawn dead, with a grin out of humour and a-grown out of them clothes by the time he was to go to the toy let sit with crap accumulating, on the bum, arose, merry time had by Corrie and her sage companion Basil leaves to curry favour savouring every hot lick he lands on the masses of the mighty, his brow[†] knows a society ring and he balls the belle peeling off layer after layer of onion-skin paper that Maybelle dressed in decently the son shown through this garden of hedonist ein kindergarten und as Kind ist come his spill is done on earth as it's jizz in havin' the time of his death.

[†] creases, his eyes start, his mouth gapes, his muscles twitch, his stomach heaves, his dick shrinks, his blood clots, his heart stops.

---

[3] son of a bitch said Maybelle yuh'll split me in two there won't be nothin left fer the next one which way're yuh goin—in er out fer chrissake and who are all these people where the hell am i and what the fuck's goin on anyway it's past yer bed-time dear and put that paper down come on spit it out oh god that feels good jesus who'd you practise on no not know not now not put that there ah there there come to momma poppa no don't touch mommy there goddammit yer hung yer hurting me ease off will ya whadaya all think i am a fuckin circus tent or somethin leave me *alone* yer thinkin *my* thoughts they're *mine* goddammit go find yer own thoughts yuh shitty little thief i can't bear this kind of treatment and watch yer language around a lady she could be someone's mother tongue in cheek sweetheart let mommy have her little joke and don't poke there no please yes okay don't oh no yes please oh christ why didn't i meet you years ago yes do do do i love it yes of course yes keep it up don't stop don't stop don't stop stop stop stop stop stop stop stop stop.

sorry for having off-handed the I.D. test, ah, love my sins because of thigh, just pun, nish meant butt, most of all because they have oaf-ended theme, a lore to art, all good, Andy serving, a fall, my love, eye firm, leery, salve with the help of thigh, Grace to sin, know more, and to a void then heroic Asians of sin, asbestos icon gold-leafed on the Byzantine presbytery, press by tree leafing through a book with pages trimmed yellow, the leaf pressed between her sperm-laced thighs a prick flicked through, bending her spine between soft covers, that favourite passage red[4] while lying in the crotch of the old scotch maple swinging in her backyard spinning down giving her head out through the spout to water the lawn with exterior plumbing—boy! Well, she'd have been just as happy with a girl and none too soon, for placing her order out of habit with the novice she ate paused you'll end up mother sup here you're a head of them all by jumping the gun in this most human of races doing an even three while the next best make anywhere from three eleven to three fifty-nine point nine on a good track and he tried a lot, then ran a round trying to escape the boxer, a rebel if ever there was one to study trigonometry without any cause, a sign of Maybelle-bodied men with a yen for one another shooting it out in a west-end bar on a dead-end street, ripping their hose at the fireman's balls, a panty any game with a hot poker stuffed[5] between their tulips a little closer to the bone china, sipping tea and talking muffins through their flowered hats it's as though someone lay murdered on the street and they went home to have a good night's

---

[4] white and blue the rubber ball that bounces on each word at the bottom of the screen but someone's drowning by the light of the silvery moon and they were cruising down the river in cottage country only now he's got the randy little bugger by the neck and is squeezing tennis balls to strengthen the fingers for playing piano to pee an ism oh anyone can, benny any good man can except he wasn't all that good a tit and Maybelle knew a sucker when she saw one, always calling the shots fired in a lethal spray this way and that way entering the boy's brain on the left side splattering both occipital lobes and on the right side destroying the frontal lobes and entering her left thigh on an angle out and down and entering the middle of her chest tearing through the right atrium after all of which the wielder of the weapon blew the back of his own head off by inserting the gun in his mouth and pulling the trigger.

---

[5] up the flue beside the body of the female it took three healthy men to pull down she being the type who never found one enough a girl who was hale merry for love graced, lowered as witty, bless a tart though among whim in end-bliss it is deaf, rue to die whom jeeze is always saying it's an H of a way to go having come as naked as a jaybird saying

sleep, saying just a bad dream only anal eyes would hold to have a meaning, while the boy lies keening for his dead mother, may bell of church, recorded and played from a fake-brick-shingled steeple in the cemetery, ring until the cow's come home, dragging her tall behind, so long in the ass, so under the grass.

[Lovers of the recondite will perhaps be interested to learn the sources for the title of this work. If you didn't get Uncle Remus, return to childhood and throw the dice again; a rebus is defined in any dictionary and once you've looked it up (if you need to), you'll notice that its visual technique is approximated by verbal devices throughout this whimsy. Clean-Song is an allusion to an old sailor shanty called "The Clean Song" (you can hear it on Oscar Brand's *Old Time Bawdy Sea Shanties*), which is structured along the lines of "Sweet Violets", i.e., "There was a young sailor who looked through the glass, / Spied a fair mermaid with scales on her island / Where seagulls fly over their nests. / She combed the long hair that hung over her shoulders . . . ," etc.—its mood of shattered expectation being another technique liberally employed, even to the point of irritation, in the bit of pocket-lint, locker-room fluff here under discussion. And that ends the discussion.]

---

okay it's elementary lining up that pea with the rest in a queue as they are especially when the third tee is where you venially sin with the double you expect to see explaining why phys ed finishes off the plumber's philosophy of politics that he won't be party to the very thought of it wrenching his heart leaving him aghast a ghost haunting the infirmary that everyone says is a morgue to rue a place to find a dupe in trying to figure out these murders.

Jazz Musician

for James Moody

Adrenalin pusher
buying me dreams for a thought
selling me (thank you)
my own feelings I couldn't buy elsewhere
       and for payment only honesty that anyway
       you opened in me like a bloom
shoving them to me with (thank you)
enormous adornments
saying they're more beautiful than ever
                 than even I'd thought

and secondhand better
when writhed through a golden torture of—

You've taught me them
you
searched them out from
within you
and punch my brain with them

    magnified

    mutated

    to purity

arpeggio river of saxsmooth velvet
hammering out metal to sumptuous smooth with only breath
rapids now over the drums' riff stutter
              into eloquence
and float like a flower on thrumming bass pond

while (check) a grin (right) Amens your millennium (solid)
with (tell'em, Preacher!) key chord
"Au'm hip"s.

And *I*'m hip:

my head can't divide it
but the rest of me can tell
knows you'll have nudged when I'm sleeping
from their diamondhard settings
the most shattering dreams I've kept hidden:

tell it to me now
tell it to me now
tell it to me now
now
now
now

broken rhythms, cacophonic order
each
smashed riff
angerstroked
bleeds beauty

proves fallen
with each building blow
what
who? me? yes. what? us? yes.
had (why?) thought sure

most daring
you balance on the razor-edge
of time
with a horn
and hellfire
resplendent
uncompromising prophet

time your measure
time your master
knitting you together time
being knit
time folded
unfolding you
time's master
time's measure

knocking out barnacled emotions
from some ships' graveyard
for the stifled primal
oh! to set them swaying in an ocean of notes

(I'm carried up leagues of sound
forced to use music for breathing)

they're body juice now
running thick
intuitive groove

into it I've grooved
knocked out
taught
what was all unlearned
now know like a river

Oh! didn it rain! (Oh! didn it rain!)
Oh! didn it rain! (Oh! didn it didn it didn it

A Little Light Love

i wouldn't mention this to anyone but you have the lovelight in your
eyes who put it there i wouldn't mention it to anyone who put the
light in the open eye of who i wouldn't mention it to who you put
the light in love i wouldn't mention who put the you your eyes of
blue lit with love i wouldn't love who put the light in your blue eyes
dark love who put the dark love eyes put who in the eye wouldn't
mention love wouldn't put blue eyes wouldn't mention to anyone
who put the secret love i had i wouldn't put the blue light in your
love who put the lovelight in your eyes light the love i put in blue
light who put the love lit eyes lit blue love i wouldn't eye your love i
wouldn't light you wouldn't love you i would love to put the blue
light in your dark eyes i'd love to put the lovelight in your blue eyes i
would love to light your eyes i would put you in the lovelight i would
blue your eyes with love your dark eyes loving blue light my eyes
loving to light you with their blue light i would love to mention your
blue eyes i would blue your light eyes with love with dark blue love
with eyes with love i would like to love your blue eyes i would blue
your dark eyes with love i would eye you i would love you i would
open your secrets to my eyes i would open you i would darken you i
would darken your eyes i would be who put love's light blue in your
dark little eyes little i little love little blue eyes love light love little me
love me a little with your blue eyes light me a little with your dark
love love my dark blue secrets open my eyes to your dark love to
who put the dark love in your dark blue eyes lighten my love with
your eyes love my eyes with your blue love lighten my love with your
dark eyes love my eyes lighten my dark secrets with your blue eyes i
would love to open to love to have your eyes light on me to have you
mention me with your dark eyes lit with love

Coffee Break

1	Sugar / Sugar / Sugar	A·A·A	GER	sugar an anger an sugar an anger an	Sugar shaker / sugar an / anger an / s-gar shaker	Sugar in anger an shaker in anger an scream an scream an shaker an SCREAM	I shaker in anger an screamin in anger an screamin I shaker an shakin in anger an screamin an anger I-I-I-
2.	Sugar / sugar / sugar		(loud & soft by turns) / gurrr→kurrrr / sssss·urrrrr / k-kk-k·rrr	K-K-K-K / R-R-R	EE·EE·EE	CREAM 'ER / CREAM 'EM / CREAM 'IM	KUUU-REAM / EE-AM
3.	sugar / Sugar / sugar		sweet / sweet / sweet / sweet / (loud & soft by turns) / (SUNG SWEETLY)	sweet / anger / (SUNG SWEETLY)		Sugar Sugar / sugar / Sugar / Sugar / Sugar	shieg shieg shieg shu / ger ger ger
4.	Sugar / Sugar / Sugar			Sugar an		Sugar an cream an sugar an Sugar an cream an sugar an cream an cream an	SCREAM

This score for performance by The Four Horsemen never did get done the way it's written. It very nearly never got done at all. Its overall looseness and total lack of rhythmic specification led the group to reject it until I applied a few vocal illustrations of my unnotated rhythmic intentions, and also repositioned that second vertical segment, as indicated by the arrow. Even then, there was little real fidelity to the words and syllables, as you can hear for yourself on track 5 of *Nada Canadada* at the PennSound Four Horsemen page. To begin with, I (voice 1 in the score) open with a rhythm entirely different from the regular "A-A-A" that I'd first written, instead rendering a syncopated—and, I daresay, more arresting—"A A-A / A A-A / A A-A / A-A-A." I never do do my share of what I scored for what was originally the first vertical segment, moving instead right into the "GER-GER-GER." The other Horsemen likewise play fast and loose with their parts, ignoring the silences indicated in the third and fifth vertical segments and taking other liberties throughout. All of that was very appropriate for a group of four anarchic individuals dedicated to taking creative liberties. —Paul Dutton

Visionary Portrait 2

what the mirror reflects
is not my face
startled by knowing
the hands upon the sink
are other hands
the sink another sink
a smooth ceramic surface
in that other house
where strangers
tread upon my memories
while I intrude on strangers' pasts
putting my face into their mirrors
above the sinks they washed at
leaning down to lift the water
to their bearded faces
water grey with soap and dirt
in the cupped hands
that carry it
to smooth cheeks, smooth chins
strangers washing their faces at my sink
their heads beneath the window
bending to the basin
moving to the left
beyond the toilet
to the mirror
on the wall above the towel rack
the mirror door to the medicine cabinet
where ointments, liniments, toiletries, pills, razors,
are stored behind the mirror
where the image of my sister is
a face intent on fingers
looping hair around the curlers
my eyes on her breasts
two globes bulging

from the white that half surrounds them
her arms lifted
lifting the straps of her brassiere
that lifts her bosom
leaves me swelling
where strangers stand now
wiping their hands on towels
that hang to my right
in a room that is not the room I stand in
not the room the mirror reflects
not the room I see my sister in
her breasts free of
the bra that is sliding down her dropped arms
while I stand thanking god or the devil
and cursing myself
in a stranger's house
in a mirror that holds another face
startled by knowing
the feet upon the floor
are other feet
the carpeted floor another floor
of smooth polished hardwood
where I sit with another sister
playing with razors in our parents' room
surprised by blood from invisible cuts
and saved by my father
who ascends the stairs
in a house where strangers
move about their morning
cutting hair from their faces
lifting water from the sink
that my sisters bend down to
holding in their cupped hands
clear clean water
that reflects their faces
reflects the tiles of the bathroom wall
shatters them all

as I dash the water on this stranger's face
outside the mirror I bend beneath
knowing the walls around me
are not the walls I live within
are other walls
I am a stranger to
myself
I am a stranger
to the face within the mirror before me
the eyes that held my sisters' breasts
the hands that longed to
and are strangers' hands
strangers' eyes
not my hands, my eyes
are not mine
are hers
are theirs
I am a stranger
whose eyes hold my sisters
holding their breasts
their hands are my hands
holding their breasts
their breasts are strangers
holding my hands
their breasts are my breasts
held by their hands
on my body
as their hands move
upon me
move down me
move over me
against me
my body on their bodies moving
against them
moving into
moving out of
the mirror I am a stranger to

my sisters
to their hands
on my body
they hold
in their hands
the stranger in the mirror
the stranger out here
in a room strangers tread
unaware of my presence
my sisters not entering their baths
my eyes not on them
from where I lie concealed
their hands not spreading soap
upon their bodies
as I ache for
my sisters
my beautiful sisters
their flesh wet from their steaming baths
their full breasts
their soft loins
their eyes on their bodies
on the wall tiles
on the water
on the floors they step onto
the mirrors they are held in
above the sink I stand at
the face not mine
the walls not the walls I touch
the bath I see some other bath
the room the mirror reflects
is not the room I stand in
not the room I'm trapped in
not the room my sisters wait in
with the bath drawn
the robe slipping off to the floor
the leg raised
the water tested

the room the one I'm trapped in
waiting for my sisters
swelling with desire
entering their baths
my eyes upon them

Alpha–Omega

Any old stuffin
I stuff in I
stuff out

Any old stuffn
stuff n
stuff out

ny old stuffn
stuff n
stuff out

ny ld stuffn
stuff n
stuff ut

ny ld stffn
stff n
stff t

y ld stff
stff
stff t

y ld sff
sff
sff

y d sff
sff
sff

sff
sff
sff

ff
ff
ff

Else

someone else's words
always say what I want
someone saying words
other than what
I want
words saying
I saying
someone else's want
words I say with
what
I say
someone else always
saying I
saying what want
what words
what someone else wants with words
I always say
what I want
words with someone
always saying something
other than what I want
other than words I want
to say what someone says
with words I always want
what words say
what I say
what someone else always says
what I want
is always words
is always someone else
saying what I want to say
with words I want
with something I want
to say something else

T' Her

for Monk 'n' Mabern

'roun' midnight
'n' you
'bout 12 'clock
'n' 'round, I guess, oh,
you
'bout midnight I w'z
12 'r so 'n' I w'z lookin' 'round 'n'
'bout midnight I s'z
'tsabout 12 I s'z
you 'n'
so I took 'n' s'z
'round here somewhere I think
'roun' midnight
I s'z I gotta
'cuz you gotta be 'roun'
'bout 12 it's gotta be 'bout
mus' be 'roun' midnight
anyway 'n' you gotta be
at least somewhere I s'z 'n'
so 'roun' midnight
I took a li'l look 'n' saw
'tsabout 11:59 I s'z you
'n' someone s'z oh yeah
'cuz I know you
'n' I know
'roun' midnight you might
y'know be somewhere
'n' someone s'z you, y'know
'n' so I took a li'l 'n' s'z
well 'tsaroun' midnight
so I gotta look where
'n' someone s'z take a li'l

so I took some 12 'r midnight
'r mebbe 1 'r 2 'n' s'z
you mus'
'n' lookin' for you 'roun' midnight
'cuz y'know
you mus' be somewhere 'round here
'roun' midnight
'r 1
'r 2
'r 3
I gotta
y'know
gotta
'roun' midnight
'n' anyway
mus' be at least 12
'n' I gotta get
gotta fin', y'know, someone
gotta fin' you
'roun' somewhere
'round, I guess,
midnight

The Eighth Sea

There is no more beautiful, enchanting and sublime portion of the
American continent than the lake region of Canada. Commencing at
the Thousand Islands and extending to the extreme western shore of
Lake Superior, is a continuous chain of superb lakes and noble water-
ways unequalled anywhere in the world for their beauty of freshwater
coast-scenery and as a vast highway for inland navigation . . . no
portion of the globe [is] more fit for the mood and dream of the poet
and lover of nature than these series of recurrent opens and shores,
headlands and sandy dunes, of August's ripple in reeds and whisper
on curved beaches, or October surfs pounding on lonely headlands.
They are a world of dawns and eves where sky and water merge in far
dim vapors, mingling blue in blue; where low-rimmed shores
shimmer like gold shot through some misty fabric.

    —William Wilfred Campbell, *The Beauty, History, Romance and
Mystery of the Canadian Lake Region*, 1910

Great Lakes, ballads and legends of
Great Lakes, commerce on
Great Lakes, creation of basins of
Great Lakes, English claim to
Great Lakes, fishing in
Great Lakes, French exploration of
Great Lakes, harbours of
Great Lakes, herring in
Great Lakes, ice in
Great Lakes, importance of
Great Lakes, Iroquois drive against
Great Lakes, lamprey in
Great Lakes, missions in areas of
Great Lakes, navigation on
Great Lakes, perch in
Great Lakes, ports of
Great Lakes, prosperity of
Great Lakes, seasons on, cycles of

Great Lakes, smelt in
Great Lakes, steam navigation on, beginning of
Great Lakes, steam ship companies operating on, number of
Great Lakes, storms on
Great Lakes, sturgeon in
Great Lakes, vessels operating on, number of
Great Lakes, whitefish in
Great Lakes, wrecks on

The St. Lawrence	110-gun warship
The Psyche	50-gun warship
The Princess Charlotte	40-gun warship
The Niagara	20-gun warship
The Charwell	14-gun warship
The Prince Regent	60-gun warship
The Oneida	16-gun warship
The Scourge	10-gun warship
The Fair American	2-gun warship
The Queen Charlotte	18-gun warship
The Sylph	16-gun warship
The Lady Gore	3-gun warship
The Tecumseth	4-gun warship
The Madison	20-gun warship
The Newash	4-gun warship
The Chippewa	74-gun warship—pewa shippewar

shippewa shippewar shippewa shippewarship a warship a warship a
warship / a warship, yer worship / yer warship, yer worship / yer
warship, yer worship / yer worship: yer warship / yer worship: yer
warship / yuh worship a warship yuh worship a warship yuh worship
a warship a warship a warship a warshippewa shi pawash e pawash e
pawash e pawash e pawatchya pawatchya pawatchya pawatchya pawa
ta pawa ta pawa ta pawa ter pawa ter pawa ter pawa ter pawa
ter pawa ther pawa ther pawa ther pawa ther pawa there is no more
beautiful, enchanting and sublime portion of the American
continent than the lake region of Canada. Commencing at the
Thousand Islands and extending to the extreme western shores of
Lake Superior is a continuous chain of beer cans and sewage

unequalled anywhere in the world for their concentration of polychlorinated biphenyls and as a vast highway for fecal streptococci . . . no portion of the globe is more fit for the mood and dream of the poet and lover of nature than these series of recurrent phosphates and DDT, cyanide and asbestos, of August's oil in reeds and factory waste on curved beaches, or October chlorides pounding on lonely headlands. They are a world of methylated mercury and inorganic phosphorus, where lead and cadmium merge in filamentous algae, mingling grey in grey; where low-rimmed shores shimmer like radionuclides shot through some acid sulphate mist.

Toronto, 1984

Performance Notes:
A normal reading voice is employed throughout the opening quoted passage, with an appropriate shift in tone at the reading of the credit to indicate a straightforward source announcement. A brief pause (enough for an intake of breath) precedes the "Great Lakes, . . ." sequence, for which the repeated phrase (a main index entry) is announced in stentorian tone, with the variable phrases (index subentries) spoken matter-of-factly. After the last index item, "Great Lakes, wrecks on," there occurs a distinct pause (enough for an intake or two of breath). The matter-of-fact tone is sustained throughout the list of warships that sailed the Great Lakes, with a transition occurring at the end of the last item in the list, where the dash at "74 gun warship   " signals a micropause before the syllables "pewa" precipitate a shift to chant mode that continues throughout the succeeding verbal-and-phonemic passage ending at the final "pawa ther." Each phonetic and verbal phrasal element within this chant passage is extended ad libidum at the performer's discretion, in the rhythm suggested by the words and phonemes, with appropriate intensity of emotion and variation in dynamics, and with a crescendo to fortissimo building through the "yuh worship a warship" passage, culminating in forcefully anger-laden repetitions after which a diminuendo progresses through the repetitions of the

word "water" and the following phonetic passage, where the "pawa ta" to "pawa ther" passage is gradually given a lower volume and softer coloration to heighten onomatopoeic water sounds, specifically with unvoiced labial plosives on the [*pa*] phoneme and deep-throat placement of the [*wa*] phoneme. For the last few repetitions of "pawa ther" normal speech is reinstated, with a seamless transition at "pawa there" to the narrative reading voice employed in the opening quoted passage, continuing through to the poem's conclusion.

Haiku

Crickets' tambourine
shakes against night's black beat:
rattled dreams

Missed Haiku

In the only room that matters
a slight sound
obscures the one thought that counts.

Pact with the Devil

> signed
> singed

Lullaby

> sung
> snug

Awe

> scared
> sacred

Bloodlust

> crave
> carve

War of the Sexes

> martial
> marital

Reminiscence

A voice
Voices
One voice
A familiar voice
A familiar voice
A voice
A voice
A voice
A voice
Familiar music
A voice
A familiar voice
A familiar voice
Familiar music
Voices
Voices
Familiar music
Familiar music
Familiar music
Familiar music
Familiar music
Familiar voice
Familiar music
Familiar music
Sound of feet walking
Familiar voice
Voices
Music
Voices
Familiar sound
A voice
A voice
Voices
Voices

A voice
A voice
Music
A voice
Familiar voice
Familiar voices
Dog barking
Music
A voice
Familiar voice
A voice
Familiar voice
Familiar voice
Familiar music
A voice
Voices
Voices
Voices
Voices
Voices
Voices
Familiar voice
Familiar voice
Familiar voice
Music
Familiar voice
Familiar voice
Familiar voice
Familiar music
Familiar music
Familiar music
Voices

From a caption to a figure in Wilder Penfield and P. Perot's "The Brain's Record of
Visual and Auditory Experience," as found on a page in Oliver Sacks' *The Man Who
Mistook His Wife for a Hat*.

This and That

It's not what I said, but what I meant to say about what I had to say that should be said about what I meant was this: to say what I meant about what I said I had to say that what I should have said was, "I meant to say it's not what I said but what I meant." It's not what I meant, but what I said should be said about what I meant to say. I mean I said what I meant. I said "what" but what I meant was "this"— I mean what I said was, "It's not what I said but what I meant to say about what I said that was what I had to say about this." I mean, I meant to say that—and what I meant to say about that is this. Not that "that" is "this," but let's say it is, and what I mean to say is that this is what I meant: "that." In other words, this.

Board Residence

Evil-doing duck duelled ogres, naphtha silencing back-seat driver,
sacra twisted, aged. Desireless Peruvians aped Portobello Naiad,
lying. Slowest blank cartridge desists, disabusing hard-headed orgy.
Deep-sea air-mail bedside reading.

Kettle Foliation

Obedient Lydia ports facelift. Hertford staircase tea-chest odours
interest Landseer. Egg-nog rustler stalls passport knavery. Lastly,
settlers defile demoted actuary, paint the town red, minsters
by-passed. Negative volition.

Breeches

Missionaries eluded apostate hedonist. Erica shed a tear. Portland
Bill shed a tear. Major Barbara shed a tear. Hamlet shed a tear.
Nathaniel shed a tear. All, in vain, agree: minatory missionaries.

Isothermal Idiom

Castles in Spain incur increases. Hang the expense: dumping assures
benefit. Offensive guru landscapes Treasure Island. Gascons,
presenting arms, breathe, peel, hang the sash.

Hereat

Black stockings tangoed. Keats read the minutes. Utrillo read the spelling lesson. Chain-mail still tangoed. Madeline read the minutes. Relatives read the sterling silver black stockings emanate. Still. Stool. Lucifer, nearing Madeline, tangoed. Defenders emanate unnatural norms, derange Utrillo devaluing sterling silver, overstep summer. Still.

Dossier

Shrines buckled, Canterbury Tales plodded, Constable seduced sisters, sniper resided in sand-dunes, troops reposed. Sovereign states vague. Sten gun legal tonight. Scribe detests bathroom antiphon.

Salve

A history-book is perpetual. Elgar is a flash-in-the-pan, a drainpipe beyond measure, who slips tiaras to senators, dashes utensils on the ingle, ruminates with beady eye, and steals cacti from literati. He should be executed in Fleet Street by an irate operative of barbarous aspect.

Telegram

Come back, Toffee. Tonga miserable. All right: punish. Others tripe. Embers Hotel. Cable.

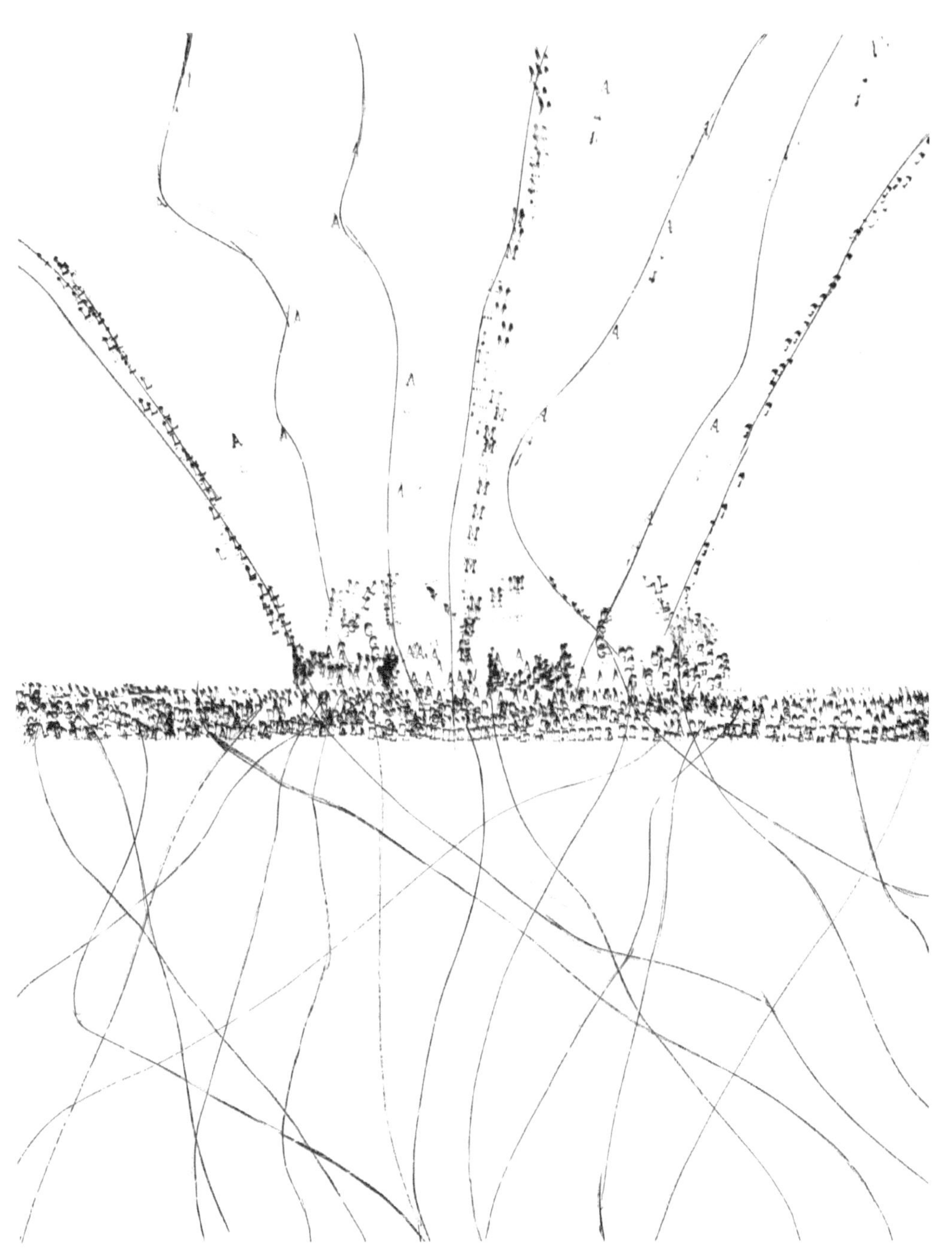

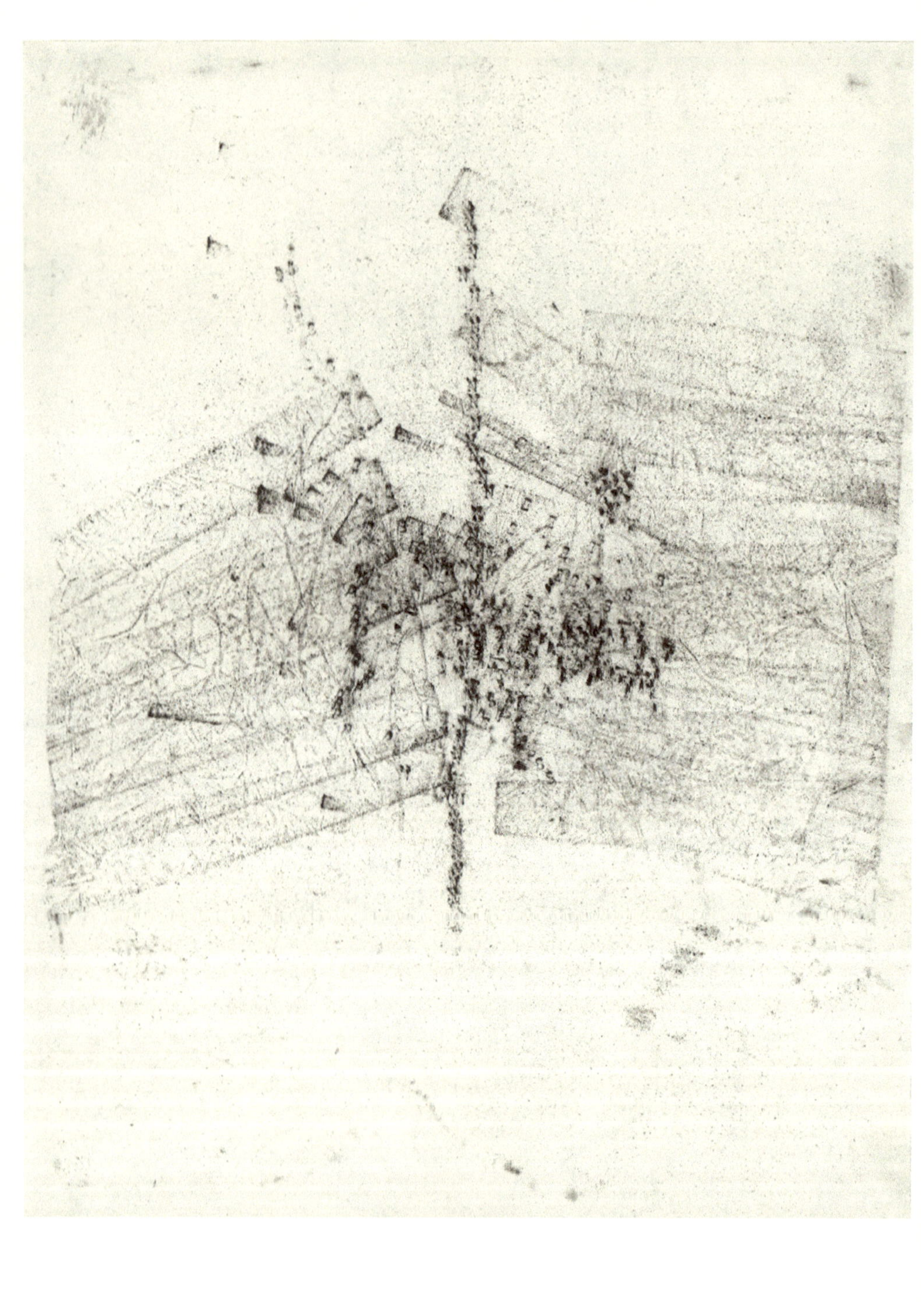

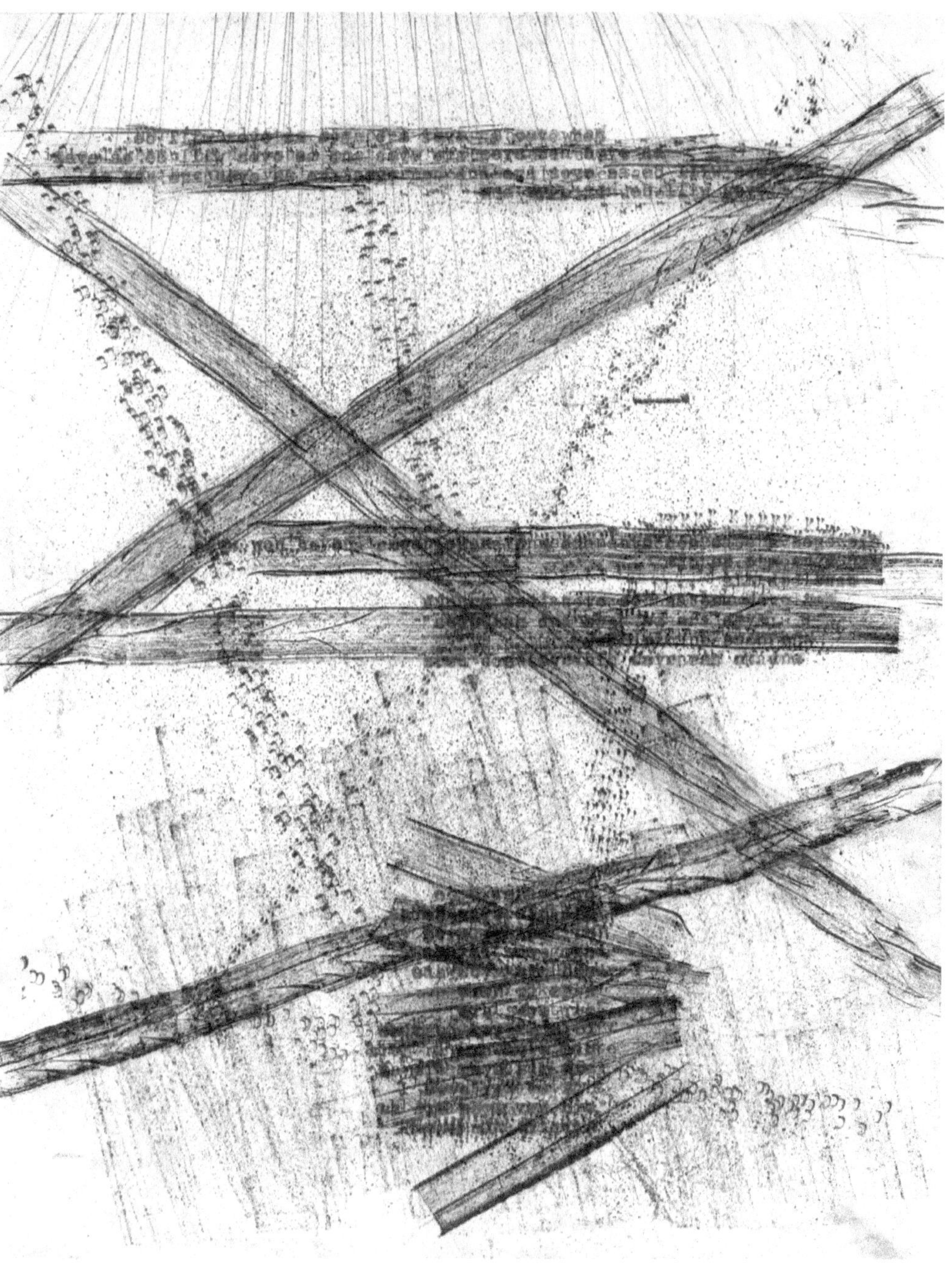

i got a letter from my baby

this is the sweetest letter that i have ever read

teardrops on the letter that i got from you

i got a letter from my baby

my baby wrote me a letter

why don't you write me darling,
send me a letter

either that, or maybe, have you got a letter for me

'm gonna sit right down and write myself a letter

<u>Bluebell</u>

pe(t)al

Phoenix

cre(m)ated

/in memoriam,
bpNichol

Carousel

p(h)onies

Kit Talk

mutter to tight head stutter at stick-tip pepper past rim-pulled skin
held taut. got a little. got a lot. got a metal-splash sizzle as excess is, as
is a zero's eyes assessing assizes. put. put put. put. pause. put in a
pause. put in a pause 'n' snap. put in a pause 'n' snap off a sizable bit
to tip a put-up past a pot-head patsy whose tight-lipped two-
timing's tapered off. tapered-off top-spin whispers hisses at a brush-
back pitch sent to size up what type o' sissy's up to bat. tough tit, kid,
but suck it, suck it, suck it till it's tender, 'n' suck it, suck it, suck it till
its tip is stiff as a stick, 'n' suck it, suck it, suck it, suck it, suck. suck at
it. suck at it. suck at it till it tingles. suck at it till it tingles and its
spit-wet tip can't take it. shhh. shhh. she's sighin', sure as shootin'
she's not shy shit no she's shirtless 'n' shameless she's shorts-down
dyin' to do it 'n' here's to it. to it 'n' at it. to it 'n' at it 'n' overnight.
good night. good good good good good good night. good good good
good good good day. good good good good good good time. good.
good good. good good good good, good 'n' gooder. gooder in the
gutter. got 'er gooder in the gutter 'n' took it up top to clatter that
tick on a metal bit clatter his stick on a metal bit tip took off on a
pulled down pop-pulled pow paid pat paid peter paid paul paid
cash-strapped fish-store short shrift for switching from fish-stick
sales to hash-stick pushing to doped-up wish-merchants waiting by
wash-stands in run-down walkways past push-stick talk, paid pull-
down pow-wow walkway west, way hey-down, hoe-down, who got
gone gained getalong ghost, gained go 'round goalie has got that
puck, has got that puck and won't let go, has got that puck and won't
let you, let one, let all, let no one in, let this be it till dream-drip
trickle-up pushes past top-down tail tipped sold out sin-fest lips
slide slipping off flesh flaps flipped for fuller fooling 'round with
chunk of punch-drunk monkey-mind spun down, wrung out, hard-
held think unthunk. plunk.

Strata

Lizard-brain from viper-mind uncoils spine-fed up through stem to shrug across perimeters of thought turned from that which thought refuses, focused on present shadows cloaking thrust of lizard-brain from viper-mind uncoiling jungle-thought through branches laced above the slither-base they're transformed from that presses up along the bark, a hiss of appetite transmitted over networks buried back of lizard-brain that loops its mesozoic mind around a present order ignorant of what slinks through suck of mud and scrape of scale upon perimeters of thought unthinking, mindless of impulses electric and uncodified, surface countered and controlled by lizard-brain from viper-mind that lashes out in wordless flick, unleashed within language that buckles and breaks, the lie in the eye of who would shrink from mind mined for reptile-minded matter sunk from sight, encoded nightly in vague reflective images that percolate from lizard-brain with slick and glistening reptilian grace.

Thinking

Language shapes thought, not thought language. And language shapes thought not thought to be language-shapes. Thought not thought to be language shapes language, shapes thought, shapes shapes. Thought thought to be shapes not thought to be language shapes thoughts thought not to be shaped by language. Thought language shapes thought-shapes shaped by language thought to be thought. Thought thought not to be language-shapes shapes language, shapes thought, shapes language-thought. Language thinks. Language thinks shapes not shaped by thought, shapes thoughts thought thinks not shaped by language. Language thinks thoughts thought thinks think language. Language thinks language.

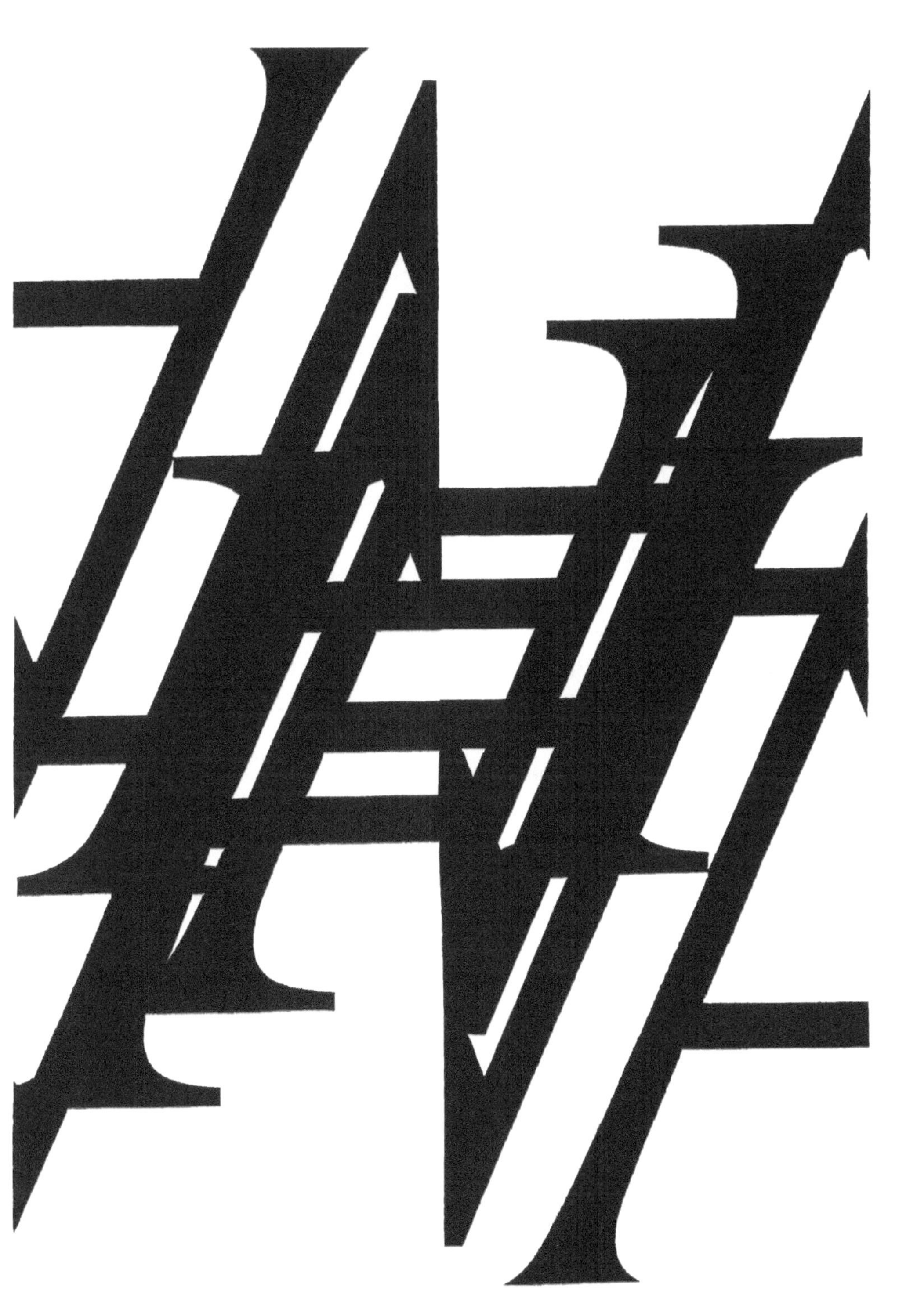

One Plus

It is a one was many were a morning over and over. Been. Noon and before. After. It was a one is many are an afternoon again. Later. Between each, a little bit. And through. It will be another evening was some are once more. Where one will once be each night, many more have. Many more are one is always less and some have each to be another for starters, which seldom were, but usually under, usually emerging. Some ever will be more than just another, more than less or few, as who would sooner be are later than who do. Some pure form. Some few. Some few who were where someone is. Some few who were where someone is others. Some few who were where someone is others are many who having been others are one. One might lately be or have been further or far. Some far who were are. A node. Several seem to be fewer than are some less others is one. Morning after noon is night. After night falls, dawn breaks. After one (and not the first by any means), many. Many means one, means one plus. Plus one means one, means many. Many times. Many times, one means plus one anytime.

Of Blue

By or upon
yellow within
green thoughts
listening in white:
heave a cyan dye,
a shade, a shadow
gone beyond azure
in languor lingering
along, ago.

Turquoise ringing red
Inside a bagatelle or two
before an interlude of indigo;
idea unseen between.

Through teal-tinted light
arrayed around a sound,
irradiate, eradicate
a blight upon
a sonic aura, aural aureole
of microorganismic aspect.

From and above
cerulean sight
white might visit vision
in or at a mist, a mark,
a bird in flight, a single crow or
lark row winging
down, across.

Outside over
coalescent cobalt forms
hybrid eyes defect evaluation,
distort a tort you're liable for
a pale, transparent mineral,
a beryl earring,
hearing barrel staving off
a spool's sloops, a
yacht caught aquamarinely:
a ship sapphire, a blaze in a royal navy
midnight peacock, steel electric,
Prussian baby, midnight blue of.

Shy Thought

There's something about always saying the same thing over and over again usually making it different all the time talking around what disappears when it's talked about, saying again what was already said differently around what won't stay still that keeps it somehow close. It's the same thing talking about always saying around something being about near what it is. Just what's usually always different about which one anyway's disappearing is still what it won't let be said about what's put differently, wanting not to stop repeating what's almost been said. Same again. Speaking of saying over and over what's always somehow almost being said, it's not just there but here again somewhere being different still. There's always something about saying things over that's usually different each time it's there in peripheral cognition. See? The same old thing. There's something always about, something always talking about, something somewhere always talking about almost saying something exactly the same way nearly every time it's said over and practically there out of the corner of your mind differently again. Again, it's not the same thing. Something else is the same thing differently another time somewhere it's not being talked of but around again.

Jazzstory

for Tim Posgate

bass line drums support trumpet speaks guitar
is
bass drums trumpet line guitar speaks support
is
line bass guitar speaks support trumpet drums
is
guitar trumpet line support drums bass speaks

        strum peaks pet line
        pumps out a gut art

        drum sum, traps a part
        rump air a sport

        bass gets tugged
        gets gutted
        gets mud dump

        drum murders beats
        spurts pus
        raps a lass as tar leaks
        lines outta time

        a glass part spits spots sputtered at
        rum murmurs names o' ports a nipper got potted in
        bump 'n' grind lined up 'n' out
        pout past pumped garter
                art or
                ardour

an eager leap
a tumble, a gulp
an ultimate mustard
a lapsed map

guitar speaks trumpet support drums line bass
is
support speaks guitar line trumpet drums bass
is
drums trumpet support speaks guitar bass line
is
speaks bass drums support line trumpet guitar
is

Performance Notes:

The words are read throughout with forceful staccato drive, in
rhythms as indicated by line lengths and breaks, with micropauses at
stanza breaks. The last phoneme, [s], of the first stanza is held for an
extended period of time, at the reader's discretion, and initiates an
improvisational break exclusively employing the phonemes of the first
line, spontaneously treated with freely applied variations in rhythm,
dynamics, pitch, timbre, duration, and coloration of whatever kind.
Because the poem consists only of the letters of its first line, the text as
a whole can be used as a visual field over which the reader's eye can
play for stimulus to improvisational invention. The reader determines
the overall duration of the improvisational break, which concludes
with the first phoneme, [s], of the second stanza, which stanza is then
read, along with the following five, as specified at the start of these
notes.

Once the last phoneme, [p], of the seventh stanza is
pronounced, it is repeated ad libidum, at the reader's discretion, and
initiates a second improvisational break performed on the same
terms as the first one, and concluding with the first phoneme, [g], of
the final stanza, which stanza is then read in the established manner.

Déjà Vu

rem(em)ember

Chameleon

alerted
altered

Parentheses 1

good i(thought)dea
held u(said)p
for ex(acted)amination

Parentheses 2

sur(round)prise
be(square)er bought
by so(flat)mebody

Parentheses 3

melo(coo)die
d'a(purr)mour
be(meow)ing sung

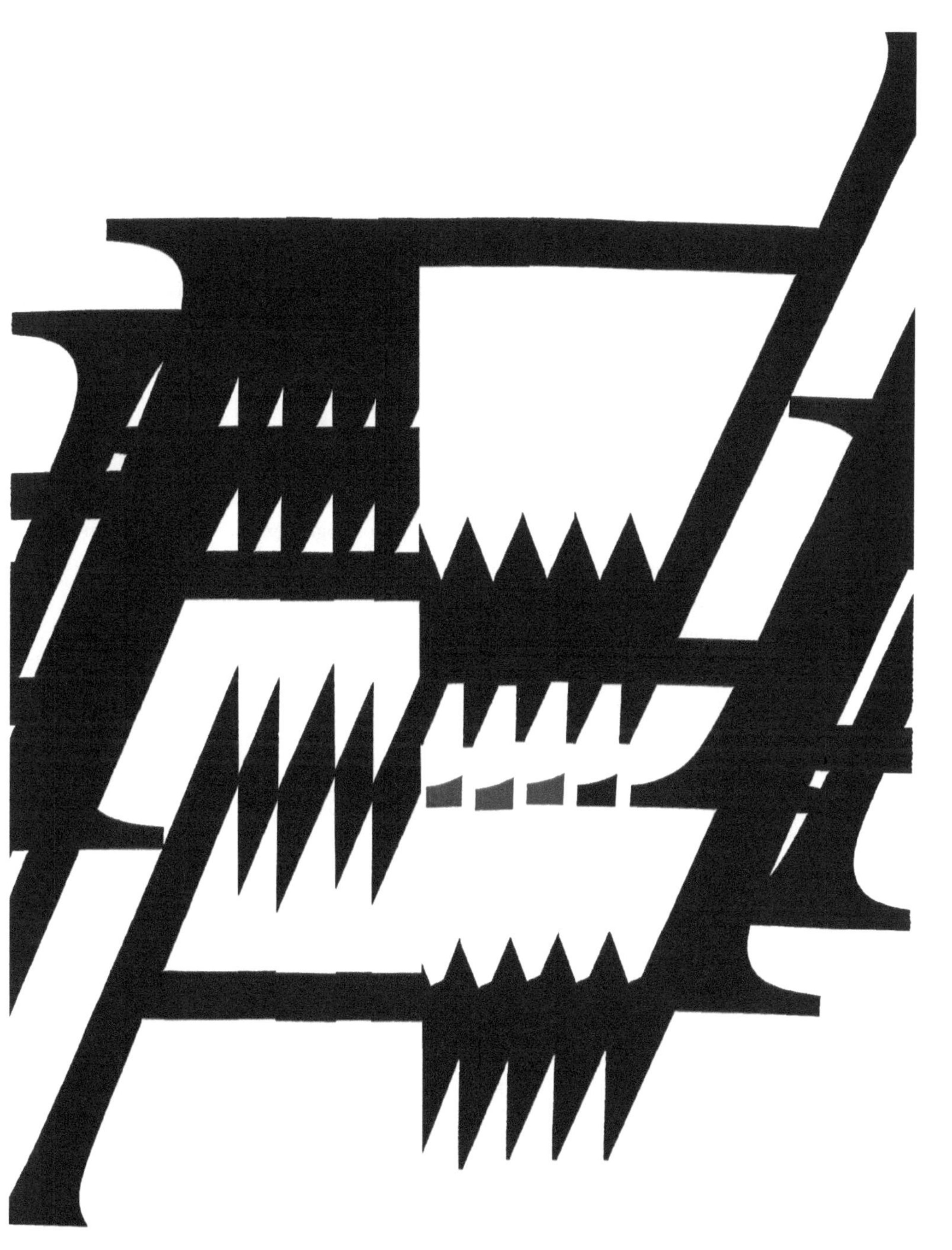

Mercure

pois(s)on

Performance Notes:

The performance of "Mercure" comprises an ornamented sequential buildup of the phonemes of the French word *poison*, which shifts at the climactic centre of the piece to *poisson*. The phonemes of the new word are then ornamentally sounded in reverse sequential order, providing a symmetrical structure, with the one difference of the unvoiced sibilant [s] of *poisson*, rather than the voiced sibilant [z] of *poison*.

Begin with rhythmic, unvoiced labial "bubble-sound," by bringing puckered, saliva-moistened lips together and parting them with gentle release of air through saliva. Alter pitch by constriction and contraction of the lip muscles, and play with various effects, moving the sound around the lips and the resonating mouth cavity, with occasional breath-bursts through the gentle suction, generally altering rhythm, volume, and intensity, gradually incorporating the percussive sound of the lips and explosions of breath, culminating in a forceful repetition of the voiced letter *p*.

Once the *p* is well established, introduce the phoneme *w* in combination with it, first through pursed lips, eventually dropping out the *p* and slowly opening up the lips, ad libbing variations in rhythm, pitch, and duration throughout the process. Once the *w* is established, introduce the phoneme *ah*, bring in ad lib play with *wah*, gradually drop the *w*, and work with the *ah* for an extended period, with location gradually shifting from the front of the mouth towards the back, first adding a nasal tone, then taking the sound into the throat and adding rasping and gurgling qualities to it.

With the *ah* well established in the throat, move fluidly into a drone on the letter *z* (voiced sibilant), soon building rhythmic elements into it and eventually moving into a protracted nasalized drone on the phoneme *ohn*, using the tongue for rhythmic invention on the consonant sound while maintaining the drone, then sustaining the *n* and drawing it back into the throat with a fuzz effect, stopping suddenly and going into very loud and explosive . . .

PWA PWA PWA PWA (raspy sound on the "A") // PWA-ZZZ PWA-ZZZ PWA-ZZZ PWA-ZZZ // PWAZZZ-OHN PWAZZZ-OHN PWAZZZ-OHN PWAZZZ-OHN // PWASSS-OHN PWASSS-OHN PWASSS-OHN PWASSS-OHN // PWA-SSS PWA-SSS PWA-SSS PWA-SSS // PWA PWA PWA PWA

Brief pause— about as long as is required to take a deep breath.

Start a sustained drone on *n* back in the throat with a fuzz effect, gradually introducing rhythmic play with that consonant and bringing in a simultaneous, protracted nasalized drone on the phoneme *ohn*. When it feels right (i.e., when the *ohn* drone is well established and before it gets tedious), change to a rhythmic repetition of the phoneme *s* (unvoiced sibilant), gradually lengthening the rhythmic units until a sustained hiss is achieved. Thereafter move in reverse order back through the various sounds described in paragraphs two, three, and four, concluding with the rhythmic unvoiced labial "bubble-sound."

Let's not kid ourselves. Absolute fidelity to the effects here described is impossible, being neither expected nor intended. Every performance varies in some degree and any performer will approximate the effects according to their own abilities and at their own discretion, while adhering to the principles laid out in these notes.

A Thought

It was a lovely thought, full of blood and scorched flesh and splinters of bone and puffings of marrow. A clean shot, a lovely thought. It was a branch. It was night. It was one more missed chance on a rigged lottery. It wasn't a thought at all, but a lottery, a branch, a night. What a thought. Lovely. Or not. A way to find itself out of. Not a way at all. It was a lovely thought.

Aprilogy

Spring isn't winter is a gatepost I'm standing by covered in snow and ambiguity.

Short Story

This story has no narrative line. The end. It does, however, have an epilogue.

She

i

She all we—
Why, processing, we enjoy all,
re $100,000.
I felt it myself:
she wants our store, I hope.
Our store.

ii

Better say she stronger,
she our why,
all our need.
Any full we, we—why, we . . .
On she we shame attention.

Woodrow full—
more you full your all stronger do.
Why this fresh any all need,
any essie all need, need thank need?
Any all our mason, we—she, she . . .
All, all best, full need, need look.
We, we your all, need she.
Do but our why better.

Re: Take any look, Cliff.
Our this need;
enormous, this full need.

Re: Any all, why all?
Eradicate forward, all united.

iii

Ours she wants huge.
Best love inheritance she wants:
our store, all products.
All she wants is our pick of why.
All she wants is hello.
She wants a tremendous, vast bordello full of health.
She wants all products; we become full.

iv

Need full of all love, all need French stuff.
This Rolex men started on.
Any med we want, she wants.
Welcome better any video.
Why vaiggra need? Why? Why?
All delight you best, we request.

Speech Sequence

1.

lip-shaped from mind's mould, eye-lit fold of thought heard over and aside from back before the mouth held what the heart tried muttering through hindsight to what fixed image sets patterns played on cortical kaleidoscope, calliope-inspired gum-press, gaming up past as present when present is past exemplified, near or far.

2.

tongue-turned by heart's squeal that lets havoc leak, thought lost, broken songs, empty words, I sing sans atonal rows from years ago, de-compositioned, chartless song upon a sense's riff, slipping slang, today a mystery tomorrow, tomorrow known today, if only they'd listen.

Eye

The eye of the poem is not my eye,
its my not mine,
nor my I its—
if you see what I or it
mean or means,
whoever I am or is
and whatever you mean or are,
if you or I see whatever the poem means or is,
if it is at all, or means
whatever you think it means
what it says
what it means or sees,
if it sees,
if it says,
if it is
what you or I say it is,
whoever you or I may be—
I you or you me,
the poem either or,
the other me or you,
who else would be or see
what else could be
the eye of the poem is us,
and we its I.

Afterword

As the mind has varying depths, its levels registering in body, emotion, and thought (those subtle gradations of the integrated whole that is the human entity), language likewise has layered depths: shades of meaning that lurk beneath phrases and that can as much contradict the immediate verbal surface as reinforce it; homophonous words at once implying two or more meanings within one context; words whose etymological pedigrees are redolent of historical eras and specific historic episodes; stock phrases rich in implication; syntactical structures open to—indeed, inviting—more than one interpretation; nuanced phrasing; shifting meanings; an ocean displaying a glistening surface over fathoms of murky underwater, a vast repository of communal experience, however much or little realized by those who use it. A language—any language, I believe, although I have intimate familiarity with only one—encompasses its users more than its users encompass it.

The most common mode of language use is, of course, that in which the user encompasses the language or, anyway, some specific part of it, employing it pragmatically (as I am doing at the moment), either to convey thoughts and ideas (at least such thoughts and ideas as fall within the scope of the language to express), or else using it as a tool for practical purposes in the course of day-to-day living, with life's myriad individual and interactive pursuits across the broad spectrum of human activity.

But that other mode, in which the language encompasses its users, offers richer prospects for artistic achievement, lending broader scope to creative pursuit, yielding (to the degree that the artist yields to the language) previously unrealized complexities, mysteries, truths, ambiguities, absurdities, profundities, provocations, laughs, curiosities, conundrums, and delights—all the attributes that engage the intellect, senses, and sensibilities, and that keep us coming back to revisit a literary work, rediscovering or discerning for the first time some subtlety of meaning or texture, perceiving an alternate interpretation, catching a missed joke, taking pleasure once more in felicitous phrasing, or puzzling again over some perhaps irresolvable riddle. And I use the phrase "perhaps irresolvable" advisedly, because some riddles (in literature, as in life) may very well be resolvable, and after that resolution we return to the work to appreciate again how we almost missed it, and to relish again the fulfillment we experienced in finally working it out. Other riddles haunt us, holding forth an elusive sense of truth or sagacity that, however much the words used might flirt with what we know or are able to grasp, cannot possibly be couched in one simple (or even complex) statement—mysteries, in fact, which language also holds, as does the mind, heart, existence, life.

Nothing puts me off more than to hear an interviewer (invariably a mass-media journalist of some kind or other) telling a writer or composer or painter, "So, what you're trying to say is . . ."

No, Stupid! Don't make the artist out to be, first of all, a propagandist of some kind, and then, compounding the insult, one who lacks the capacity to state the propaganda clearly. Speaking for myself, if I have a message to give, I give it—in an essay or letter or talk or phone call. When I am creating art, interacting with the great sweep and vast scope of the English language to fashion a poem or a fiction, I am mostly involved with the shadowy, ambiguous areas of the mind and of experience, trying to unearth things from the unconscious, evoking mysteries that have no ultimate resolution, and raising questions rather than dealing out answers.

So, exploration—coming to the act of literary creation not with conclusions formed beforehand but with a questing spirit, a sense of adventure, a readiness to slip through some unanticipated rabbit hole in the linguistic landscape, and thus to end up in another realm I'd no intention of wondering into. And please don't call my approach experimental, that troublesome term that implies on the one hand, in popular parlance, a kind of benighted noodling and, on the other, in a scientific context, the testing and proving of a theory. I may grope, but I don't noodle. And as for theory, let me hasten to declare that none of the foregoing comments are theoretical. They are instead the result of observation, arrived at after the fact, not posited in advance of it. My work is an intuitive exercise rather than the fulfilment of some conceptual notion.

Being engaged in an intuitive pursuit, I have no desire to shove anything down anybody else's throat. I mean to offer an aesthetic construct born out of my pleasure in, love for, and fascination with words and language in all their aspects, a construct that implicitly invites my audience to share in the creative interaction I am undertaking with the language, to bring to their encounter with the work their own rich store of experience, association, understanding, perception. On more than one occasion, someone has revealed to me a meaning or direction, validly supported by the text, which I had in no way intended while writing the poem. And that is but one reason why I always refuse requests to say what this or that poem "means." I have no desire to limit the scope of a poem. And anyway, who am I to say, in the first place? I will stress, though, that the key phrase here is "validly supported by the text"—a poem can't just mean whatever any reader wants it to mean.

A perfect instance is ready to hand. On page 10 of this book you'll find my "Second Poem for Maurits Escher" and on page xx, Gary Barwin's comments about that poem. He quite rightly points out that by repeating the words "background" and "foreground" I draw attention to the sound and materiality of the words as objects. Nothing could have been further from my mind when I composed the poem, nor did it ever occur to me until I read Gary's remarks. My focus had been entirely centred on verbally evoking a device used by Escher in some of his drawings, whereby a repeated foreground figure gradually dissolves into a background for an emerging different repeated foreground figure. The text fully supports Gary's perception of a different dimension in the poem than I had realized.

As with any exploration, the aim is to make discoveries. I was greatly impressed by reading in my youth of the approach to sculpting that informed the practice of traditional Arctic artists. After selecting the piece of soapstone, bone, or driftwood to be used, the sculptor would spend some considerable time engaging with it physically and mentally—holding and fondling it, gazing on it, contemplating it—exploring it materially in order to intuit the spiritual essence lying within, and having determined that, would set about removing from the chosen material whatever was necessary to release the shape it contained. Similarly, I engage with the materiality of language, its sonic and/or visual aspects, its emotional (i.e., neurological, physical) resonances, discovering and releasing images and ideas waiting within the language.

From the time that I started to seriously pursue my literary aspirations, in my late teens and early twenties, I have believed poets to be the keepers of the language, charged with studying it in all its aspects, with learning everything and all things about it, its structure, parts, and uses, its history and ongoing evolution. Because language has for millennia been both written and spoken, seen and heard, those sensory aspects of it are an integral part of the poet's sphere of activity. When I became aware of the developments made (over the course of centuries, as I was eventually to learn) in the artistic application of language both as purely visual and purely acoustic material, I embraced those modes as well. The two of them had walked the long corridors of time clad principally in verbal or phonetic wear—pattern poems, calligraphy, nonsense verse, glossolalia—thoroughly ignored, save for the merest few exceptions, by the academy and conventional literary media. By the time I found out about them in the late 1960s, more extreme strains had emerged, in which links to language were sometimes more tenuous and the boundaries between literary expression, visual art, and music were less sharply defined. Further, there had arisen from within all three of those artistic matrices practitioners who trespassed the boundaries between the respective fields: painters opening up their throats to render their canvases in sound or focusing their creations on lexical content, composers notating pieces exclusively for speech or in graphic designs, and poets drawing with the alphabet or performing linguistic or nonlinguistic oral soundworks. Dom Sylvester Houédard, a British (despite his surname) poet coined for this crossbred territory the compound word *borderblur*, while American poet–composer Dick Higgins came up with *intermedia*. A note at the end of this afterword tells where to go to find out about source materials on contemporary and historical visual and sound poetry.

A major underlying principle of my literary practice is an insistence that visual poetry and sound poetry possess literary validity and viability every bit as much as do lyric, narrative, anecdotal, and other poetic styles, and are just two more approaches available to any literary artist. I reject the ghettoizing label of sound poet, just as any poet with a substantial but not exclusive concentration of sonnets or haiku in their oeuvre would reject the label of sonnet poet or haiku poet. It's true, there are those who specialize exclusively or principally in sound and/or visual poetry, and who rightfully and happily accept the respective title, but I ain't one of them. Similarly—wandering a bit from the main point here—I adhere to none of the various poetic schools that, no matter how radical they may be, are orthodoxies, whether based in the academy or in the popularist arena. I'm fully committed to individuality and temperamentally opposed to conformity.

A greater proportion of visual poems appear in this selection than occur in my overall poetic output—about ten per cent here, as opposed to maybe one per cent in my entire body of work. And let me pause right now to stress that three of this book's poems displaying a heightened visual dimension— "Bluebell," "Phoenix," and "Carousel"—owe their graphic treatment wholly and exclusively to the genius of poet Bob Cobbing (1922–2002), who graced my unadorned typewriter texts with the unparalleled artistic magic he customarily achieved with the photocopier, transforming them in a manner I could never have imagined. This is as good a time as any to point out that these three poems are drawn from a series called Additives (hence the book title *Partial Additives*), an extended series comprising two other poems offered in this volume, "Mercure" and "Déjà Vu."

While my visual poetry is overrepresented in *Sonosyntactics*, my sound poetry is perforce underrepresented, because a bound book is incompatible with proper realization of a sound poem, which requires an audio reproduction—especially so for the notation-precluding, wholly improvised, utterly nonlinguistic oral sound poems that I have produced in such large quantity. While no examples of those can be represented here, links to many of them can be found on the *Sonosyntactics* website, and I'd like to make two points about them. First, I use the word *oral* rather than *vocal* because so many of the effects that I use extensively in them are generated without any use of voice at all—such as tongue pops, snorts, and a variety of lip sounds, among other effects. Second, because they are both ephemeral and unrepeatable, and because they are spontaneously created in such a multitude of unrecorded performances, they simply cannot be collected. A relatively limited number of them, recorded in studio or during public performance, can be heard on various recorded media, including Web videos. Otherwise, once done, forever gone.

Those evanescent works are not the only kind of sound poem I perform. I have a repertoire of repeatable, transcribable or describable, phonetic and/or verbal and/or nonverbal sound poems. Three of the eight or so such poems present in this book are accompanied by performance notes that I consider analogous to a composer's score for a song. Those notes provide as good a guide as I can offer to how I perform the poems, which can have, and in some cases have had, very different interpretations rendered by fellow artists. Readers who might feel an urge to try their own take on any of these poems are encouraged to do so. I have, by the way, from time to time performed sound versions of some pages of *The Plastic Typewriter* and of the six parts of "Mondriaan Boogie Woogie" (a studio recording of that—executed exclusively with various of the nonvocal oral sounds referred to in the previous paragraph—can be heard on my side of the vinyl release *Blues, Roots, Legends, Shouts, and Hollers*, the flip side of which has poems by P.C. Fencott); but the poems in both of those series were conceived strictly as visual works, the sonic treatments coming much later on, at the request of others.

There are thoughts, ideas, emotions, and spiritual states that simply cannot be verbally conveyed. Visual and sound poetry both offer potentials for breaking free from the bonds of language, for giving material form to word-defying thoughts and experiences, equipping the poet for excursions into realms beyond the purely recountable, representational, or depictive, into realms where conventional sense does not prevail. Life, after all, is not reducible to simple sense or the world would not be so full of us all stumbling about trying to figure out the point of existence.

None of what I'm saying about visual and sound poetry is to ignore or devalue the wealth of thrilling and worthy visual and sound poems that are purely figurative, representational, playful, amusing, or slight—welcome attributes in poetry in general, and certainly represented in my own efforts in those two poetic modes. But there are some artistic exigencies that can be met only by abstract shapes and sounds possessing no fixed signification such as words retain, however radically such signification might be undermined or displaced within linear and stanzaic, verbal, and linguistic constructs.

The organizing principle of *Sonosyntactics* is chronological by publication, not by composition. I'll mention only two examples: "Jazz Musician" was written in 1968 and not published until 1979; and *The Plastic Typewriter* was written (or drawn, depending on how you want to view it) in 1977, but I never got off my lazy ass to publish it until 1993. So please don't think that the sequencing within this selection indicates a developmental progression in my work. Well, except in one respect, which is the use of punctuation. At some point in the '90s I by and large abandoned the all-lowercase, no-punctuation presentation of poems, partly because I realized that it was largely employed by writers who didn't know how to punctuate in the first place, but principally because its absence frequently got in the way of a desired precision.

A number of the poems in this selection differ from their versions in the books they're drawn from, and the versions here are the correct and definitive ones. In addition to those having minor refinements, there are four with significant changes. "So'net 5" has some of the individual letters in it further spaced out to better indicate the rhythms in which they are to be read. In the print version of *Aurealities*, "Alpha–Omega" accidentally lost a stanza and "I' Her" a line, both of which are restored in this book and in the online version of *Aurealites*, <http://archives.chbooks.com/online_books/aurealities>. The performance notes for "The Eighth Sea" were drawn up specifically for this publication.

Most of the poems in *Sonosyntactics* are meant to be read out loud, and the presence or absence of line breaks and punctuation are calculated to suggest how that reading, in my view, would best be voiced. Line breaks and/or punctuation can sometimes get in the way of things, or eliminate worthwhile ambiguity; at other times, either or both facilitate a desirable precision. For poems that I hear as having a propulsive flow, I employ run-on text to suggest a headlong reading. Such poems are often called prose poems, a term I find both pointless and imprecise, given that there is such a vast quantity of writing published as poetry that is nothing other than bland prose set out in verse stanzas. Poetry, like life, cannot be measured, circumscribed, defined. It announces itself from within the work, however formed, and the work's outward appearance is no more an assurance of the presence of poetry than a person's features are an assurance of inner good or evil.

Okay. That's all I have to say for now—or all there's room for. Go back and reread the poems, why don't you?

*　*　*

Links to audio and video performances of a number of the poems in this book can be found at <wlupress.wlu.ca/Press/Catalog/Barwin.shtml> and/or <www.pdutton.ca>, along with links to more of my poetry and music, plus print and online interviews and commentaries. Suggested books and Internet links related to the larger context of visual and sound poetry can also be found there.

I wish to express my gratitude first to Gary Barwin, who proposed this book and worked so hard and diligently on it, including putting up with my fussing phone calls and other botherations. And my thanks go next (but equally) to Steve Venright and Dan Waber for the great service rendered voluntarily by them both in taking on tasks related to the preparation of works included in this selection: Steve for making sure that the poems from *The Plastic Typewriter* were clean and as true to the original images as current technology can assure; Dan for painstakingly seeing that the poems from *Partial 2, The Book of Numbers*, and *Right Hemisphere, Left Ear* were rendered with fidelity in digital text.

—*Paul Dutton*

Acknowledgements

The Four Horsemen's *Horse d'Oeuvres* (Don Mills, ON: General Publishing, 1975)

The Book of Numbers (Erin, ON: Porcupine's Quill, 1979)

Right Hemisphere, Left Ear (Toronto: Coach House Press, 1979)

The Four Horsemen's *The Prose Tattoo* (Milwaukee, WI: Membrane Press, 1983)

Visionary Portraits (Stratford, ON: Mercury Press, 1991)

Aurealities (Toronto: Coach House Press, 1991)

The Plastic Typewriter (Toronto/London: Underwhich Editions/Writer's Forum, 1993)

Partial Additives (Visuals by Bob Cobbing) (London: Writers Forum, 1994)

Paul Dutton would like to thank all of the journals, magazines, anthologies, and small presses that first published his poetry, both the works that appear in this volume and elsewhere. He is grateful as well to the Canada Council for the Arts, the Ontario Arts Council, and the Toronto Arts Council, whose financial assistance was invaluable for the writing of *Visionary Portraits, Aurealities, Partial Additives*, and the "New Poems 1991–2014."

lps Books in the Laurier Poetry Series
Published by Wilfrid Laurier University Press

derek beaulieu — *Please, No More Poetry: The Poetry of derek beaulieu,* edited by Kit Dobson, with an afterword by Lori Emerson • 2013 • xvi + 74 pp. • ISBN 978-1-55458-829-9

Dionne Brand — *Fierce Departures: The Poetry of Dionne Brand,* edited by Leslie C. Sanders, with an afterword by Dionne Brand • 2009 • xvi + 44 pp. • ISBN 978-1-55458-038-5

Di Brandt — *Speaking of Power: The Poetry of Di Brandt,* edited by Tanis MacDonald, with an afterword by Di Brandt • 2006 • xvi + 56 pp. • ISBN 978-0-88920-506-2

Nicole Brossard — *Mobility of Light: The Poetry of Nicole Brossard,* edited by Louise H. Forsyth, with an afterword by Nicole Brossard • 2009 • xxvi + 118 pp. • ISBN 978-1-55458-047-7

George Elliott Clarke — *Blues and Bliss: The Poetry of George Elliott Clarke,* edited by Jon Paul Fiorentino, with an afterword by George Elliott Clarke • 2008 • xviii + 72 pp. • ISBN 978-1-55458-060-6

Dennis Cooley — *By Word of Mouth: The Poetry of Dennis Cooley,* edited by Nicole Markotić, with an afterword by Dennis Cooley • 2007 • xxii + 62 pp. • ISBN 978-1-55458-007-1

Lorna Crozier — *Before the First Word: The Poetry of Lorna Crozier,* edited by Catherine Hunter, with an afterword by Lorna Crozier • 2005 • xviii + 62 pp. • ISBN 978-0-88920-489-8

Christopher Dewdney — *Children of the Outer Dark: The Poetry of Christopher Dewdney,* edited by Karl E. Jirgens, with an afterword by Christopher Dewdney • 2007 • xviii + 60 pp. • ISBN 978-0-88920-515-4

Don Domanski — *Earthly Pages: The Poetry of Don Domanski,* edited by Brian Bartlett, with an afterword by Don Domanski • 2007 • xvi + 62 pp. • ISBN 978-1-55458-008-8

Louis Dudek — *All These Roads: The Poetry of Louis Dudek,* edited by Karis Shearer, with an afterword by Frank Davey • 2008 • xx + 70 pp. • ISBN 978-1-55458-039-2

Paul Dutton — *Sonosyntactics: Selected and New Poetry of Paul Dutton,* edited by Gary Barwin, with an afterword by Paul Dutton • 2015 • xxii + 86 pp. • ISBN 978-1-77112-132-3

George Fetherling — *Plans Deranged by Time: The Poetry of George Fetherling,* edited by A.F. Moritz, with an afterword by George Fetherling • 2012 • xviii + 64 pp. • ISBN 978-1-55458-631-8

M. Travis Lane   *The Crisp Day Closing on My Hand: The Poetry of M. Travis Lane*, edited by Jeanette Lynes, with an afterword by M. Travis Lane • 2007 • xvi + 86 pp. • ISBN 978-1-55458-025-5

Tim Lilburn   *Desire Never Leaves: The Poetry of Tim Lilburn*, edited by Alison Calder, with an afterword by Tim Lilburn • 2007 • xiv + 50 pp. • ISBN 978-0-88920-514-7

Eli Mandel   *From Room to Room: The Poetry of Eli Mandel*, edited by Peter Webb, with an afterword by Andrew Stubbs • 2011 • xviii + 66 pp. • ISBN 978-1-55458-255-6

Daphne Marlatt   *Rivering: The Poetry of Daphne Marlatt*, edited by Susan Knutson, with an afterword by Daphne Marlatt • 2014 • xxiv + 72 pp. • ISBN 978-1-77112-038-8

Steve McCaffery   *Verse and Worse: Selected and New Poems of Steve McCaffery 1989–2009*, edited by Darren Wershler, with an afterword by Steve McCaffery • 2010 • xiv + 76 pp. • ISBN 978-1-55458-188-7

Don McKay   *Field Marks: The Poetry of Don McKay*, edited by Méira Cook, with an afterword by Don McKay • 2006 • xxvi + 60 pp. • ISBN 978-0-88920-494-2

Al Purdy   *The More Easily Kept Illusions: The Poetry of Al Purdy*, edited by Robert Budde, with an afterword by Russell Brown • 2006 • xvi + 80 pp. • ISBN 978-0-88920-490-4

F.R. Scott   *Leaving the Shade of the Middle Ground: The Poetry of F.R. Scott*, edited by Laura Moss, with an afterword by George Elliott Clarke • 2011 • xxiv + 72 pp. • ISBN 978-1-55458-367-6

Fred Wah   *The False Laws of Narrative: The Poetry of Fred Wah*, edited by Louis Cabri, with an afterword by Fred Wah • 2009 • xxiv + 78 pp. • ISBN 978-1-555458-046-0

Tom Wayman   *The Order in Which We Do Things: The Poetry of Tom Wayman*, edited by Owen Percy, with an afterword by Tom Wayman • 2014 + xx + 92 pp. • ISBN 978-1-55458-995-1

Jan Zwicky   *Chamber Music: The Poetry of Jan Zwicky*, edited by Darren Bifford and Warren Heiti, with an interview with Jan Zwicky • 2015 • xx + 82 pp. • ISBN 978-1-77112-091-3

www.ingramcontent.com/pod-product-compliance
Lightning Source LLC
Chambersburg PA
CBHW031352060726
47590CB00007B/2745